REFLECTIONS ON GOD

"Mark Wade has presented a thoughtful and spiritual work that leads people on a spiritual journey. His guide encourages the reader to find hope and direction in the midst of these very uncertain times. This devotional guide will help both groups and individuals to find strength in our Lord and Savior Jesus Christ."

Reverend Dr. Michael A. Evans, Sr.
Bethlehem Baptist Church
Mansfield, TX

"Mark Wade has fashioned an encouraging practical and motivational guide for persons who are ready to discover a more intimate relationship with God. The carefully crafted plan for spiritual formation described in *God in the Everyday*, is rooted in the author's many years of faithfully entering into a daily time of personal worship. Readers will find wisdom and valuable assistance in their journey of spiritual growth through Wade's confessional approach in his writing. Inspired by a desire to help followers of Jesus grow in faith, this book reaches consistently into scripture for its bedrock in guiding seekers. In addition, consistent with the long spiritual formation history of the Christian faith, Mark Wade seeks to help his readers in developing a growing confidence and discipline in the personal practice of prayer."

Dr. George H. Gaston, PhD
Pastor, Retired, San Antonio, TX

"What I love about this devotional workbook is that it speaks to the very essence of why we're here…experiencing God in the everyday of life. It invites the reader to build their house on solid rock, not shifting sand. It offers a blueprint for constructing a life with gold, silver and precious stones, rather than wood, hay and stubble. It makes a case for investing in eternal things and leaving a legacy for the kingdom of God. It's theologically sound, and wonderfully accessible. If you're ready to live a life of meaning and purpose, but you're not sure where to begin, let Mark coach you through the first 14 weeks. You'll be amazed at how much you can accomplish in that amount of time… and you'll be glad you did!"

Curt Grice
Associate Pastor of Spiritual Formation,
First Baptist Church Arlington

"Mark Wade has been my friend and business associate for over 20 years. After embarking on the journey, he lays out in his book, I am delighted how my relationships with family, friends and business associates are being enriched. Commitment to this plan is turning my desire to walk with God into a celebration of his love and purpose for my life."

Sam Gorman
Division Manager, National Write Your Congressman
Fort Worth, TX

"This devotional guide, *God in the Everyday*, is a helpful journey from nominal Christianity to living the way of Christ each day. The practical experience shared in Mark Wade's own journey will resonate with many people who struggle to integrate faith into daily living. The organization of the study into manageable, but significant daily steps makes it accessible to church-based small groups."

Dr. Kyle Henderson
Senior Pastor, First Baptist Church, Athens, TX

"*God in the Everyday* is a great resource for anyone wanting to develop (or sustain) the discipline of meeting with God daily. Mark Wade's posture is genuine and humble as he simply desires to pass along what has been a transformational practice for him – finding God in the everyday. This devotional book is as good as anything else we could use at First Baptist to help our people (especially young adults) grow in the area of daily time with God."

Rev. Katy Reed Hodges
Minister of Congregational Life
MDiv, Truett Seminary, Baylor University

"An incredibly helpful book for an individual, small group in a church setting, or friends who desire a study to encourage them in their spiritual formation journey. Mark Wade has prayerfully put together a book, based on scripture, that will guide the reader along a step-by-step path into a learn-as-you-study, daily progression towards spiritual maturity. This 14-week study isn't a 'do this to become more like me' read written by Mark, but instead is written from the vulnerable heart of a humble, mature layman's approach for 'everyman' who simply desires a moment-by-moment walk with Christ every…single…day."

Larry Link
Christian Adult Education Minister, Retired, Dallas, TX

"What a wonderful work! *God in the Everyday* is such a practical, straight forward and God based presentation of the gospel. It does not matter whether you are a non-Christian being presented with the gospel for the first time or you are a life-long believer, this work speaks to both and all those in between. It is filled with truth and is a great road map that leads the reader to learn skills that will enable them to be what God wants for all of us to be as we learn from Him, grow and increase in our faith so that we can be that light to the world that we all as Christians are called to be."

Randy J. Long, Attorney at Law
Long, Claypole & Blakley Law, PLC,
Enid, OK

"Here is what you can expect of *God in the Everyday*: A warmly personal, highly scriptural, well-organized pathway to a disciplined and joyful walk with God."

Dr. Dan McGee, PhD
Author, Speaker, Consultant, Edmond, OK

"In his book, *God in the Everyday*, Mark Wade accomplishes multiple challenging tasks.

1. He has distilled many of the elements of the Christian faith into a pathway for spiritual growth.

2. He has searched Scripture to make these key elements clear and grounded in God's truth.

3. He has made them understandable for the everyday person.

4. He has shown the reader an accessible pathway to daily time in God's Word and God's presence that will help create new habits for some and strengthen the habit for others.

Whether you read through the book alone or as a group study, you will be deeply blessed."

Dr. Ross O'Brien, PhD
Professor of Management and Director of the
Center for Business as Mission
Dallas Baptist University, Entrepreneur, Dallas, TX

"Mark Wade's perspective on finding God in the everyday is a tremendous blend of heartfelt reflection and meaningful application. This guided devotional leads the reader down a road that enriches your understanding on how prayer and the Word of God are to be treasured and applied in your everyday experiences. Mark's words are impactful because they are rooted in authenticity. He writes from a personal experience that serves as a model to anyone who desires to find meaning in each day. No matter your current season or circumstances, this book will help all who read it to find God in the everyday."

Jerimiah Smith
Pastor, University Baptist Church
Fort Worth, TX

"*God in the Everyday* will help you understand who God is, enjoy God, and strengthen your desire to be more like Jesus. This study points you to God's Word, the only source of truth, using a systematic disciplined approach to know God, deepen your relationship with him, and live a meaningful, fulfilling life."

Chris Adamson,
CEO, National Write Your Congressman

Dana Adamson,
Bible Study Fellowship, Rockwall, TX

"Mark Wade has beautifully encapsulated these 14 truths for seeking God in our everyday lives. This study presents relevant, real world questions and scripture-based answers as we live out our faith and build a deeper relationship with our Creator. This study is perfect for the brand new Christian, as well as the seasoned Christian, as the questions challenge the reader to go deeper in their faith at the level that God leads. I found myself spiritually challenged and greatly encouraged as I walked through *God in the Everyday*."

Jenn Kleiber
Host of the Faith Filled Entrepreneur Podcast
and Founder of Pressing Onward, LLC

"In *God in the Everyday*, Mark Wade takes his readers on a journey though the Christian life—from life's beginning at the command of God to the embrace of God that believers receive as they go Home. Individuals and study groups will benefit from Wade's writing in daily devotions and weekly meetings....Sign up for this 14-week journey!"

Dr. Mark T. Goodman
Senior Pastor, Rabbit Creek Church,
Anchorage, AK
Author of *The Ordinary Way*

"Mark Wade distills a wealth of personal, practical experience to help others take up the Christ life. If you've struggled to invite Christ into all areas of your life, or if you've never trusted Him at all, this book is a good place to begin."

Becky Jackson, DMin
Pastor, Northwest Baptist Church,
Ardmore, OK

"Mark Wade provides a profound, yet easy to follow 14-week path of transformation exploring 14 Truths that will deepen the faith and effectiveness of any Christian or open-minded seeker of truth and purpose. As our orientation guide and friend, Mark winsomely illuminates for us what a daily journey with God looks like—one that he has been personally practicing for decades—that we can emulate to both discover and live out God's purpose for us. Encouraging, challenging, relatable and transformational, *God in the Everyday* is a fulcrum for greater personal and spiritual fulfillment."

Kurt Knapton
Investor and Strategic Advisor, Realm Resources,
Arlington, TX

"'Living life with God in the everyday' should be a key phrase in all our lives. Through his 14 Truths, Mark helps us discover how to have that kind of walk with the Lord."

Dr. Chris Liebrum
Vice President, Howard Payne University,
Brownwood, TX

STEVE —   *8.1.21*

YOUR CHARACTER AND COMPETENCE IS OFF-THE CHARTS! WHICH IS WHY I TRUSTED YOU SO QUICKLY. THANK YOU FOR GIVING THIS PROJECT THE PROFESSIONALISM

GOD

in the Everyday

I WANTED IT TO HAVE. I CAN'T TELL YOU HOW MANY PEOPLE HAVE TOLD ME HOW

A 14-WEEK GUIDE TOWARD
HOPE, PURPOSE, AND FULFILLMENT

MUCH THEY LOVE THE COVER! I'M ETERNALLY GRATEFUL. PLEASE PRAY GOD

C. MARK WADE

WILL USE THIS MATERIAL TO DRAW PEOPLE INTO A HEALTHIER RELATIONSHIP WITH JESUS.

MARK
JOHN 13:34

CHOOSE COMMITMENT
MINISTRIES

Published by Choose Commitment Ministries, Arlington, TX 76017

Contact us at choosecommitment.org

Cover and Interior Design by: KUHN Design Group
Copy Edit by: Renee Crawford

Copyright © 2021 by C. Mark Wade

ISBN 978-1-7369963-0-0 (Paperback)
ISBN 978-1-7369963-1-7 (eBook)

1. Devotional 2. Bible Study 3. Discipleship 4. Mentoring 5. Self Help

This book is dedicated to my Lord and Savior, Jesus Christ.
May He use it for His glory and for His Kingdom.
I pray all who read it will be drawn to a closer,
more authentic, healthier relationship with Him, which,
in turn, will lead us toward hope, purpose, and fulfillment.

———————————

ACKNOWLEDGMENTS

Thank you to all who have believed in this project, specifically Pam, Caleb, and Taylor Wade. I'm grateful for their unwavering love and confidence in me. Honey, thank you for your contributions and insights regarding the entire book, especially on the "Day 7" content. To my parents, Charles and Rosemary Wade, for their lifelong support, encouragement, and example. To Cindy Dake, whose spiritual maturity, insight, and wisdom were on full display throughout the content development stage of this book.

CONTENTS

INTRODUCTION

It was a cold Saturday morning in February. You know, the kind where you want to stay in bed a little longer, pull the covers over your head, and sleep in. My wife, Pam, gently nudged me out of bed, because I had a commitment to fulfill that morning.

Every year, typically in late January or early February, the youth ministry of our church hosts what we call Wake Up Weekend. The purpose is to give junior high and high school students an opportunity for a first-time encounter with Jesus, or if they already know Jesus, an opportunity to develop a closer, deeper, healthier relationship with Him. Many churches have a similar event and refer to it as a Disciple Now (or DNow) weekend.

Families within our church volunteer to host groups of students in their homes for the weekend. The groups typically include eight to twelve young people from the same grade level. The students spend Friday and Saturday nights at their host homes, while Saturday is full of worship gatherings, Bible study, and mission projects around the community. All in all, they get very little sleep (by choice), and for those who host a group of boys, there are usually a few shenanigans! For the students, Wake Up Weekend is always memorable, and many students point to it as one of the highlights of their year.

For adults, however, one of the highlights of Wake Up Weekend happens on Saturday morning when the deacons of our church go to host homes to cook pancakes for the students. As the kids wake up to the smell of pancakes and bacon, we bring out plates of plain pancakes, chocolate chip pancakes, blueberry pancakes, and, my personal favorite, pancakes with real bacon bits.

For most of our thirty-six years of married life, Pam and I have hosted ninth or tenth grade boys in our home. Investing in the lives of young people has always been a priority for us, because we are both the beneficiaries of faithful men and women who invested in us as we were growing up. However, on this particularly cold Saturday morning in February, we were not hosting. As a deacon, though, I had committed to cook pancakes.

So after Pam nudged me out of bed, I dressed, gathered my pancake cooking supplies (including the bacon bits), and drove to the host home assigned to me. I flipped pancakes while talking with the boys and getting to know each of them a little better. Once they finished eating, I cleaned up my cooking area, said my goodbyes, and headed home. As I was driving, I received a phone call that would ultimately lead to the writing of this book.

"Mark, this is Don."

"Hey, Don, how are you?" It was unusual for Don to call me on a Saturday morning, even though we had been working together for about ten years. Nothing could have prepared me for what Don was about to say.

"Mark, I found out yesterday that I have stage IV leukemia," Don said in his strong, steady, eighty-four-year-old voice. "And I wanted you to know. It's going to be okay, though. God is in control, and He's got everything under control."

I wish I could remember what I said to him. I'm sure it was an attempt to comfort and speak encouragement to him. I do remember I prayed for him before we ended our call. In the silence of the drive home on that frigid Saturday morning, I was overcome with sadness. I began to think about the example Don had been to me and others on our team.

Although he was thirty years older, I was his sales manager. However, I never doubted who knew more about sales and who was teaching whom. Don had been in sales longer than I had been alive. By the time I met him, he had been a professional salesperson for roughly fifty years!

As a young man, Don started his career selling for the Fuller Brush Company. He and his wife, Geneva, had married young, and over time, they had four daughters. As families do, theirs kept growing—kids, grandkids, great-grandkids, and now great-great-grandkids were starting to join the family.

As a career salesman, Don built a long, successful career that provided well for his family. The last ten years were what brought us together on the sales team for National Write Your Congressman (NWYC). It didn't take me long to realize he had learned and forgotten more about sales than I had ever learned!

At NWYC, we both understood the roles and responsibilities we each had. Don was gracious, patient, and encouraging to me. His ego was healthy enough that, even with all of his experience, he kept learning from those around him.

As we got to know each other better, it became obvious that Don was a man of strong faith. His everyday life was guided by his walk with God. Attending Mass was a daily commitment for him, as were prayer and Scripture reading. Frequently, he would share inspirational quotes and Bible verses with me. Over time, I began to realize that the decisions he made every day were filtered through his faith. His relationship with the Lord informed and empowered his everyday life.

Don and Geneva were married for more than sixty years. I watched him care for her sensitively, sacrificially, and securely the whole time I knew him, especially in the latter years as she fought disease and dementia. On the day we buried Geneva, I watched Don with his family. Calm. Supportive. Encouraging.

In the midst of what was surely one of his deepest valleys in life, Don was secure and steady. I remember wondering, *How can he be that way on a day like this?*

Because he had been living life with God in the everyday.

Don knew God had it all under control, even in that season of loss. He had walked with His Lord long enough and consistently enough to know that he could trust God even on the day that he said goodbye to the love of his life. He knew Geneva was in a better place, finally healed, no more pain, no more disease.

Ten years of memories and moments played across my mind as I drove home on that Saturday morning. My head and my heart tried to reconcile all I had experienced with Don over the years with the realization that those moments would come to an end all too soon.

I began praying through the tumult of emotions and thoughts that followed his phone call. At some point in my conversation with God, the phrase "living life with God in the everyday" came to my mind. It was a concept I had seen lived out in Don's life for the past decade in hundreds of conversations, frequent times of prayer together, and the sharing of inspirational readings.

Don and I continued our conversations and prayers until he passed away. He approached death without any fear. He knew his destination was Heaven, and his reward was eternal life with Jesus.

On the day I said my final goodbye to my friend, I acknowledged with deep gratitude the imprint Don had left on my life as I considered how much my life and my faith had changed and grown over the last ten years.

A CHANGE IN CAREERS

Before I arrived at NWYC, I was a financial analyst with Texas Instruments (TI) for fourteen years. In the latter months of 1997 and the early months of 1998, it became clear to Pam and me that I would need to change jobs. It was time for something new. Why? Several reasons.

I had a forty-five-mile, one-way commute to TI, which could often take as long as ninety minutes to drive. Along with the demands of my work, the commute caused me to sometimes go multiple days in a row without seeing our sons, Caleb and Taylor. As a dad who intended to raise boys to be men after God's heart, I knew time with them was essential. Yet, my job frequently required me to leave the house before they awoke and return after they were asleep. While completing a writing assignment for his fourth-grade class, Caleb wrote that he didn't get to see his dad much, except on the weekends. Reading his paper, I gained insight into his perception of my absence. It cut at my heart.

While I had a little control over the growth of my income, it was fairly limited. Pam brought in some supplemental income by teaching private voice lessons, drawing on her degrees in music education and vocal performance. As we looked toward the future, we both realized the need to increase our income in order to provide for our family's needs.

Additionally, there was a growing desire in my heart for something different, maybe an opportunity to make a bigger difference. So, as followers of Christ, Pam and I began praying that God would bring us a new opportunity. What kind, we weren't sure. We just believed He had something different for us, maybe something in a sales environment.

We are big believers in the old axiom: *Pray like it all depends on God, and work like it all depends on you.* So, as we were praying, I started job hunting. I attended a job fair at the Dallas convention center in the spring of 1998. There were hundreds of companies in attendance, all looking for salespeople.

I interviewed with several companies. I sought counsel from several Christian men, whom I respected both as men of God and as businessmen. Ultimately,

I was referred to NWYC, a legislative research company. I sought them out, interviewed, and after long discussions, extensive research, and continual prayer, Pam and I felt God leading us to make a change.

I left TI and contracted with NWYC in straight commission sales, which was about as different as one can imagine from my work at TI. I quickly realized I could not do the work in my own power. Frequently, I would find my mind racing to questions like, *Will I be able to make enough sales this week to feed my family?* Anxiety caused me to focus on my needs over the needs of my prospects, and it derailed my effectiveness.

About that time, I came across the *One Year Chronological Bible* with daily Scripture reading assignments. If I followed the plan, I could read through the Bible in a year. At thirty-six years of age, I had never read through the Bible completely, and I'm ashamed to admit I had never established the habit of a consistent, daily quiet time with God.

My life changed as I began meeting with God day by day, morning by morning. I would pray, then read the Scripture passage assigned to that particular day. I learned to praise Him. I learned to ask the Holy Spirit to reveal to me what I needed to learn as I read the Bible. Bottom line, I learned to seek God every morning, to work wholeheartedly in the hours that followed, and to trust Him to provide for our family.

God began to bless my work in new ways. My career and responsibilities with NWYC began to grow and expand as I transitioned from a sales representative role into a sales leadership role. That's when Don and I began working together. It didn't take long for me to observe that Don's life had qualities I admired: calm, patience, strength, wisdom, just to name a few. While he never formally mentored me, it was our day-to-day interactions that taught me so much about what it looked like to walk with God in the everyday.

WHAT DOES THE BIBLE SAY?

Back to that cold Saturday morning in February. Once the phrase "living life with God in the everyday" came to mind, my next thought was, *I wonder what the Bible has to say. I know what I think, and I think it describes the way Don lives his life and the way I try to live mine, but what does the Bible say?* When I arrived home, I sat down and began to look in God's Word for evidence of how to live life with God in the everyday. What you will read in the following pages is a result of my search through Scripture, my journey through prayer, and my discoveries through many conversations with the Lord. I pray it will inspire and encourage you to embark upon or continue this precious journey I've come to call living life with *God in the Everyday*.

The simple truth is that we as human beings frequently try to live this life in our own power. Why? Pride, mostly. John Stott, the English Anglican priest and theologian, said, "Pride, then, is more than the first of the seven deadly sins; it is itself the essence of all sin."[1]

In our pride, we try to live life our way even though the King of kings and Lord of lords says in Matthew 11:28: "*Come to me, all you who are weary and burdened, and I will give you rest.*" And in John 8:12, Jesus says, "*I am the light of the world. Whoever follows me will never walk in darkness, but will have the light of life.*"

Jesus welcomes us into His presence at any time, at any place, and for any reason. As the apostle Paul wrote the church at Ephesus, "*we may approach God with freedom and confidence*" (Ephesians 3:12).

We don't have to live one minute of any day in our own power. His Spirit will dwell with us and teach us all things. John 14:26 is our assurance from Jesus Himself: "*But the Advocate, the Holy Spirit, whom the Father will send in my name, will teach you all things and will remind you of everything I have said to you.*"

So, again, what does the Bible say about living life with God in the everyday? Let me suggest the following 14 Truths:

- Everything begins with God.
- God gives us life.
- God gives us abilities that grow and mature.
- We recognize our sin.
- We meet Jesus.
- We choose Jesus.
- We receive the Holy Spirit.
- We receive spiritual gifts.

- We are equipped to continue the work of Jesus and grow His Kingdom.

- We exercise our gifts in obedience and love.

- We grow in the Lord, experiencing spiritual formation and maturity.

- Our gifts develop and we bear fruit.

- Our lives are characterized by the fruit of the Spirit.

- We die to live eternally with God.

My everyday journey with God has now been consistent since 1998. My work with NWYC granted me much more independence and flexibility during the work week. The quantity and quality of time with Pam and the boys increased substantially. I've watched Caleb and Taylor graduate from high school and college. Each of them is now a youth pastor, serving the Lord and their churches.

Through this life journey, God has revealed and taught me in the simple, everyday habit of meeting Him, through prayer and the reading of His Word, that living life with *God in the Everyday* has been anything but common—it has been transformative.

God invites each of us to that same transformative, secure, hope-filled life with Him in the everyday, so that we may discover the hope found only in Him, the purpose for which He created us, and the fulfillment realized in obeying Him.

TIME WITH GOD

The daily habit of communicating with God was such an important part of the spiritual breakthrough I experienced years ago. If I missed a day, I didn't beat myself up and declare my new habit a failure; I just got up the next day and resolved to meet with Him again.

As I began meeting with God every morning, my time with Him might last ten minutes, or it might last an hour. I've learned it's not so much about the *quantity* of time, as it is the *quality* of time. I would pray, read Scripture, and ask God how He wanted me to apply what I read.

Specifically, I started getting out of bed earlier than normal. I would go to my dining room, kneel down, and begin praying. I learned to offer words of praise and adoration for who God was, is, and will forever be. The Bible verses you will read in Truth 1 became part of my offering of praise as I memorized the Scriptures and offered them to Him in praise.

I would tell God that I love Him. "I Love You, Lord" by Laurie Klein would rise up out of my heart almost every morning, and I would sing it to Him.

I would ask God to teach me how to love Him and how to love others. Over time, these words started pouring out of my heart almost every morning, *All I am and all I ever want to be is Yours. Please use me for Your glory.*

Then, my prayer would transition into asking for His provision in my life and the lives of my family. Having started a straight commission sales job, most days the provision I prayed for was related to our financial position. Some days, it would be about health or relationships or wisdom or courage or strength—or all of the above! I also prayed for other people in my life who I knew had needs, and I would ask God to give provision or healing in their lives. Whatever was creating anxiety in my life, whatever was heavy on my heart, I tried to give it to Him and trust Him with it.

Then I would open my Bible to the assigned passage to read for that day. I would place my hands on the pages, ask the Holy Spirit to reveal what He wanted me to learn, and start reading. As I read, I would underline specific parts that spoke to me. I might even jot a few notes down in the margins. Some days, I would get a clear word on what I needed to learn and apply. Other days, it wasn't immediately obvious. Over time, I learned the Lord would always teach me something; it just might not be right at the moment I was reading.

Today, more than two decades later, the pattern is very similar. I don't find myself on my knees as much. The tears, though, continue to flow as I comprehend more and more fully His unending, boundless, forgiving, sacrificial love for me and all mankind!

LET'S GET STARTED

You may want to explore these 14 Truths on your own, or, as I recommend, with a small group of people. I encourage you to take one week for each of the 14 Truths. Invest six days alone with God, followed by a seventh day with a small group of people who are also studying these same 14 Truths.

Now, here's my challenge to you: In order to live life with God in the everyday, you need to develop the habit of spending time with God every day. If you miss a day, don't beat yourself up; just get up the next day and renew your commitment to daily meet with God again.

If an early morning time doesn't work for you and your schedule, find another time that does. The important part of the daily journey is to set aside some time each day to pause and spend it with God. This is sometimes referred to as the discipline of solitude.

Henri Nouwen—Catholic priest, professor, author, and theologian—wrote

> Without solitude it is virtually impossible to live a spiritual life. Solitude begins with a time and place for God, and him alone....we need to set aside a time and space to give him our undivided attention....The more we train ourselves to spend time with God, and him alone, the more...we will be able to recognize him even in the midst of a busy and active life. Once the solitude of time and space has become a solitude of the heart, we will never have to leave that solitude. We will be able to live the spiritual life in any place and any time. Thus the discipline of solitude enables us to live active lives in the world, while remaining always in the presence of the living God.[2]

I've included a day-by-day study plan as part of each week's Truth. Through this daily guideline, you will

1. **PRAY:** Pray each day and ask the Holy Spirit to reveal what He wants you to learn in your time with Him.

2. **READ:** Read the introductory comments about each Truth. Read aloud the Scripture verses from which I learned the Truth. Reading aloud engages your eyes, your tongue, and your ears, enabling you to more fully comprehend and remember what you are reading.

3. **APPLY:** Answer the questions at the end of each Truth. Identify the main lesson(s) you learned and determine the practical application for you.

4. **MEMORIZE:** Memorize a Scripture that speaks powerfully to your heart.

5. **SHARE:** Share your answers and lessons learned with others. Why is this important? The Christian life is to be lived out in community. Jesus lived in community. He chose twelve men we know as the apostles with whom He lived life and ministered. Luke writes about the birth of the church. He tells us how the body of believers *"devoted themselves to the apostles' teaching and to fellowship, to the breaking of bread and to prayer"* (Acts 2:42).

> In a small group, something special takes place that cannot happen elsewhere. A small group of caring individuals offers a safe environment in which group members can focus on the word; ask questions; share joys and struggles; know and be known; love and serve one another; and, as James 5:16 says, 'confess... sins to each other and pray for each other.' It's a place where Christians can 'work out [their] salvation with fear and trembling' (Phil 2:12). Whether in a community care group, men's group, women's group, or Sunday school class, everyone in the congregation should have a point of connection with the body through a small group.[3]

Find or form a small group of people with whom you can meet weekly to, among other things, share what you are learning and hear what they are learning. "Day 7" of the day-by-day study plan is dedicated to meeting with your small group and includes a basic outline for your time together.

If you will commit to learning more about these biblical Truths and incorporating them into your daily life, you will develop a deeper, healthier relationship with God that will improve every other relationship you have. It will move you, gradually, toward the hope, purpose, and fulfillment you desire deep down in your heart.

Are you ready? Let me offer this prayer of encouragement for you as you begin.

PRAYER OF ENCOURAGEMENT

Thank You, Lord, for life lived with You. I pray each person who reads this prayer will recognize and embrace the truth that we can come into Your presence at any time, at any place, for any reason, knowing confidently that the King of kings and the Lord of lords welcomes us with open arms. Thank You for inviting us to leave our sin, all that burdens us, overwhelms us, and defeats us at Your feet. You are the Almighty and the Everlasting. There is none other like You. You alone are worthy of all praise and honor and glory. Holy, holy, holy are You, Lord God Almighty! All nature bows in Your presence. Circumstances align themselves at Your beck and call. And one day, every knee will bow in heaven and on earth and below the earth, and every tongue will confess that Jesus Christ is Lord to the glory of God the Father. Thank You for life lived with You every single day! Teach us, Lord, how to love You with all of our hearts, souls, minds, and strength. Teach us how to love others the way You love them. Find us faithful in living such a way that the fruit of Your Spirit is on vivid display. May those with whom You connect us see You as You truly are—through our lives and our testimonies. Draw them to a healthy relationship with You, so they will bear healthy fruit and influence well for your glory. Amen.

EVERYTHING BEGINS WITH GOD

E verything?" you ask. Yes, according to the Bible, everything begins with God! Notice that Genesis 1:1 doesn't tell us who God is. Moses, as he writes Genesis, assumes we all know God. He just writes, *"In the beginning, God…"* No introduction. No explanation. Just *"In the beginning, God…"*

The apostle Paul tells us that God's invisible nature reveals Himself to us.

> *For since the creation of the world God's invisible qualities—his eternal power and divine nature—have been clearly seen, being understood from what has been made, so that people are without excuse.* (Romans 1:20)

Paul writes that no one has an excuse for not knowing God. Everything and everyone begins with God!

God spoke, and everything came into being. All nature bows in His presence. The sun rises and sets at His command, as does the moon. The stars shine with such majesty and brilliance that the naked eye sees them billions of miles away. Seas roll, rivers flow, and oceans live within their boundaries. Lightning flashes, thunder roars, and rain nourishes His creation. The fish of the sea, the birds of the air, and all creatures who move along the ground were created by God.

Consider God's highest creation: humanity. We are created by God and in His image. According to Scripture, we are wonderfully made (Psalm 139:14).

Consider a small sampling of what science has discovered so far about the wonders of the human body:

- An adult's blood vessels, laid end to end, extend approximately 528 million feet or 100,000 miles![4]

- The human nose can smell about 1 trillion different odors. And, your eyes have these muscles in them that enable both eyes to move in the same direction in a single 50-millisecond movement.[5]

- While our galaxy has roughly 300 billion stars, our bodies contain about 7 *octillion* atoms![6]

- The "gray matter" in our brains is made up of about 86 billion neurons.[7]

Wow! How is this possible?

We were created in God's image. He breathed the breath of life into us and made us for His purposes.

He is worthy of all praise and honor and glory. So, we bow before Him and praise His holy name, for there is no other name in Heaven or on earth or in hell like His! There is no other God but The God. He alone is worthy of our praise and worship. In fact, Scripture tells us that one day, "*All nations will come and worship before you, for your righteous acts have been revealed*" (Revelation 15:4).

In His Word, we discover God, in whose image we were created. If you're not sure about all of this, read God's Word. And if you're completely on board with this concept that Everything Begins with God, then you, too, read His Word!

SCRIPTURE FOR TRUTH 1:
EVERYTHING BEGINS WITH GOD

---

*Read these Scriptures and reflect upon
how Everything Begins with God.*

In the beginning God created the heavens and the earth. — Genesis 1:1

*"I am the Alpha and the Omega," says the Lord God, "who is, and who
was, and who is to come, the Almighty."* — Revelation 1:8

I AM who I AM. — Exodus 3:14

*Holy, holy, holy is the Lord God Almighty, WHO WAS, AND IS, AND
IS TO COME!* — Revelation 4:8

He is Lord of lords and King of kings. — Revelation 17:14

*I called to the LORD, who is worthy of praise, and have been saved from
my enemies.* — 2 Samuel 22:4

*You alone are the LORD. You made the heavens, even the highest heavens,
and all their starry host, the earth and all that is on it, the seas and all
that is in them. You give life to everything, and the multitudes of heaven
worship you.* — Nehemiah 9:6

*Let all the earth fear the LORD; let all the people of the world revere him.
For he spoke, and it came to be; he commanded, and it stood firm.* —
Psalm 33:8-9

*For great is the LORD and most worthy of praise; he is to be feared above
all gods.* — Psalm 96:4

*Praise be to the name of God for ever and ever; wisdom and power are
his. He changes times and seasons; he deposes kings and raises up others.
He gives wisdom to the wise and knowledge to the discerning. He reveals
deep and hidden things; he knows what lies in darkness, and light dwells
with him.* — Daniel 2:20-22

*Great and marvelous are your deeds, Lord God Almighty. Just and true
are your ways, King of the nations. Who will not fear you, Lord, and*

bring glory to your name? For you alone are holy. All nations will come and worship before you, for your righteous acts have been revealed. — Revelation 15:3-4

You are worthy, our Lord and God, to receive glory and honor and power, for you created all things, and by your will they were created and have their being. — Revelation 4:11

To him who sits on the throne and to the Lamb be praise and honor and glory and power, FOR EVER AND EVER! — Revelation 5:13

PRAY – READ – APPLY – MEMORIZE – SHARE

At the end of the introductory comments and Scripture references for each Truth, you will find a daily study guide. Use these suggestions to begin, restart, or continue your daily time with God. Every week, you will Pray – Read – Apply – Memorize – Share, as you live life with God in the everyday.

 DAY 1

Today, start your time with God in prayer. Praise God for who He is. If you have never, or if you have infrequently, offered praise, try reading aloud and offering the Scriptures for Truth 1 as a prayer of praise to God. Pray the Holy Spirit will reveal insights to you as you read the verses.

If you haven't already read through the introductory comments for Truth 1, read them now. Underline, highlight, or make notes in the margins as you read.

Read through the Scripture for Truth 1.

Close in prayer, for God is worthy of our praise, and prayer is the most intimate way for us to communicate our praise to Him.

 DAY 2

Like yesterday, start your time with God in prayer.

Read aloud the Scripture verses and reflect upon how Everything Begins with God. Which verses resonate with you most? Identify a verse to memorize this week. Write it down here and begin memorizing it.

Answer these questions. Pray and think about how you can apply them in your life.

- In what ways is it easy for you to believe everything begins with God?

- In what ways is it difficult for you to believe everything begins with God?

Close in prayer.

 **DAY 3**

Today, as you begin your time with God, ask the Holy Spirit to reveal what He wants you to learn.

Read the Scriptures and reflect upon how Everything Begins with God.

Rehearse your memory verse. Take it a sentence at a time. Read the first sentence out loud over and over until you can say it out loud without looking at it. Then, repeat this process with the second sentence. Once you can say the second sentence out loud without looking, put the first two sentences together. Once you have memorized the first two sentences, add the third sentence and so on until the entire Scripture is locked in your memory.

Answer these questions. Pray and think about how you can make applications to your life.

- Do you find anything disturbing about this week's Truth? If so, what?

- What is comforting about believing Everything Begins with God?

- How does believing that Everything Begins with God impact your ability to praise Him?

Close in prayer.

——————— DAY 4 ———————

Start your time with God today in prayer.

Read the Scripture verses and think about how Everything Begins with God.

Practice your memory verse.

Have you written a prayer of praise before? Take a few minutes to write a prayer of praise now.

Close in prayer.

——————— DAY 5 ———————

Open your time with God by praying the verse you are working to memorize this week.

Read the verses for Truth 1.

What other Scriptures do you find which teach you that Everything Begins with God? List them here.

To get you started on your search, here are some of my favorite ways to do Bible research.

- Go to openbible.info/topics. In the search line, put "God" or "God knows".

- Do you ever have questions about God and the Bible? Here is a go-to source for just about any question that comes to your mind. Go to gotquestions.org and type in "questions about God (all)" (or just type: www.gotquestions.org/questions_God.html). Each topical question has many Scripture verses in the answer section to help ground you in your Bible discovery.

- At gotquestions.org, read this question and answer: "What is the aseity of God?" In case *aseity* isn't on your daily vocabulary list (because it isn't on mine), the word means the quality or state of being self-derived or self-originated; specifically, it is the absolute self-sufficiency, independence, and autonomy of God.

- If you prefer using a Bible you can hold in your hands and you don't have a study Bible or you are looking for a new one, I recommend the NIV *Life Application Study Bible, Red Letter Edition.*

Close in prayer.

—— DAY 6 ——

You've almost wrapped up Week 1. If you have begun to establish a solid time with God every day, then I rejoice with you. If it's been a little less than regular, then I encourage you to renew your determination (as many times as it takes) to spend time with your Creator every day. Today, praise God for who He is and thank Him for the time you've spent in His presence this week. Ask God to help you adopt this new (or renewed) habit day by day.

Review your memory verse.

List one or two ways you can apply the Truth: Everything Begins with God.

    1.

    2.

On Day 4, you wrote out a prayer of praise. Who can you think of to share it with today? Why do I encourage you to share your prayer of praise with a person when it was written to God? The psalmist did the same thing—he wrote out prayers that became songs and shared them with the people of God. If you think your prayer of praise would be encouraging to someone else, share it!

Close in prayer.

—— DAY 7 ——

If you are meeting with a small group as part of this study, use this day for your group meeting.

Here is a possible outline for your time together as a group:

Open Your Hearts:

- Worship song: "So Will I (100 Billion X)" — Hillsong Worship

- PRAYER: Ask one or two people to offer their Prayer of Praise from Day 4.

- SCRIPTURE: Encourage one or two people to share the verse they memorized this week.

Discussion:

1. What do the Scriptures for Truth 1 tell us about who God is?

2. Share some of the other Scriptures you found which teach that Everything Begins with God. What do they tell us about who God is?

3. What are some roadblocks to believing Everything Begins with God?

4. What is comforting about this Truth?

5. How should this Truth affect our praise?

6. Think about your daily schedule for the upcoming week. How will your belief that Everything Begins with God impact

   - your work and interaction with coworkers?

   - your home life and how you treat your family?

   - your social life and relationships with friends?

   - the choices you make, your speech, and your actions?

Time of Commitment:

- WORSHIP SONG: "Revelation Song" — Kari Jobe

- PRAYER: One or two group members share their Prayer of Praise from Day 4.

If you are not meeting with a small group, please take time on your own to go through the small group outline.

GOD GIVES US LIFE

What were the conditions under which you were born? Some are born in the best of situations, while others are born at what may seem to be the most inopportune time or under the most difficult circumstances.

As Pam and I were expecting our first child, we decided not to learn the sex of the baby until birth. People would ask, "Do you want a boy or a girl?" At first, I would answer, "a boy." Pam typically answered, "Either is good with me." As Pam's pregnancy progressed, though, we began to answer, "You know, what we're praying for is a healthy child."

Every parent hopes for a healthy baby. Most have their hopes realized, but some do not. If you have experienced the loss of a baby prior to birth, the birth of a stillborn baby, the birth of a child who has challenges or different abilities, or the loss of a young child, my heart breaks for you and your loss.

If you are struggling with the reality of an unwanted or unplanned pregnancy, please know God's image rests upon your little baby. As painful and daunting as it may seem to bring this child into the world, God can create beauty and goodness out of what humans see as impossible circumstances. Parenthood, or the quest for parenthood, helps us realize more fully the value of life, as well as its fragile nature. The simple truth is life is an amazing, priceless gift from God!

My mom and dad were twenty-one when I was born. They had married fourteen months earlier, when they were juniors in college. My mom had an art class in the spring semester of her senior year. She had fifty art projects due over the course of that semester. On the final day of class, she presented all of her projects. Her forty-ninth project was a rolling pin with the handles painted red. Her fiftieth project was me, sitting on her lap dressed up in my Sunday best. Obviously, I was her most creative "project" of the fifty, and, of course, I earned her an A for the class!

Twenty-six years later, I watched my first son being born, and two thoughts hit me almost simultaneously: *How can a person experience the birth of a baby and not believe in God? I had no idea I could love another human being this much!* These same thoughts overwhelmed me just as profoundly when my second son was born.

Life. It's a miracle. It's a gift. The Bible tells us that we were created in the image of the Almighty God (Genesis 1:26-27); God knows us before we are born (Psalm 139:13-14); God knows the hairs on our heads (Matthew 10:30); God loves each one of us enough to die for us (Romans 5:8).

Consider this: The Creator and Sustainer of life gives us breath (Genesis 2:7). God created us exactly as He intended. He doesn't make mistakes. He created each and every one of us, and He did so for His purposes (Ephesians 2:10). One of the joys of life is learning what that purpose is for each of us.

Embrace your journey. Seek Him. Offer all you are and ever hope to be to God, and watch where He takes you. After all, He created you in His image and for His purpose!

SCRIPTURE FOR TRUTH 2:
GOD GIVES US LIFE

*Read these Scriptures and reflect
upon how God Gives Us Life.*

Then God said, "Let us make mankind in our image, in our likeness, so that they may rule over the fish in the sea and the birds in the sky, over the livestock and all the wild animals, and over all the creatures that move along the ground." So God created mankind in his own image, in the image of God he created them; male and female he created them. — Genesis 1:26-27

When God created mankind, he made them in the likeness of God. — Genesis 5:1

For in the image of God has God made mankind. — Genesis 9:6

Did not he who made me in the womb make them? Did not the same one form us both within our mothers? — Job 31:15

For you created my inmost being; you knit me together in my mother's womb. I praise you because I am fearfully and wonderfully made; your works are wonderful, I know that full well. — Psalm 139:13-14

But at the beginning of creation God "made them male and female." — Mark 10:6

PRAY – READ – APPLY – MEMORIZE – SHARE

——————— DAY 1 ———————

Start your time with God in prayer. After praising God for who He is, offer a word of thanks for your life. As good as your life may seem or as troubled as it may be right now, recognize that you are alive, and that life is an amazing gift from God. Thank Him for the lives of those you love and the people you encounter today. Thank Him for living your life with you every minute of every day. Pray the Holy Spirit will reveal insights as you read this week's verses each day.

If you haven't already read through Truth 2's introductory comments, read them now. Underline, highlight, or make notes in the margins as you read.

Read through the Scriptures for Truth 2.

Close in prayer with a heart full of thanks for the life God has given you.

——————— DAY 2 ———————

Begin your time with God in prayer. If prayer is new to you, don't overcomplicate it. Prayer, in its purest form, is simply a conversation with God. In fact, Jesus said

> *And when you pray, do not be like the hypocrites, for they love to pray standing in the synagogues and on the street corners to be seen by others. Truly I tell you, they have received their reward in full. But when you pray, go into your room, close the door and pray to your Father, who is unseen. Then your Father, who sees what is done in secret, will reward you. And when you pray, do not keep on babbling like pagans, for they think they will be heard because of their many words. Do not be like them, for your Father knows what you need before you ask him.*

> *This, then, is how you should pray:*

"Our Father in heaven, hallowed be your name, your kingdom come, your will be done, on earth as it is in heaven. Give us today our daily bread. And forgive us our debts, as we also have forgiven our debtors. And lead us not into temptation, but deliver us from the evil one." — Matthew 6:5-13

Read aloud the Scriptures for Truth 2 and reflect upon how God Gives Us Life. Which verses resonate with you most? Identify a verse to memorize this week. Write it down here and begin memorizing it.

Answer these questions. Pray and think about how you can make applications to your life.

- What were the conditions under which you were born?

- What do you think God meant when He said, *"Let us make mankind in our image"*?

Close your daily time with God in prayer.

 **DAY 3**

Today, as you begin your time with God, ask the Holy Spirit to reveal what He wants you to learn about how God Gives Us Life.

Read again the Scripture verses for this week.

Rehearse your memory verse.

Answer these questions. Pray and think about how you can make applications to your life.

- How have you seen the image of God on display within yourself?

- How do you see the image of God on display in others?

Close in prayer.

 **DAY 4**

Begin with prayer, thanking God for what He is showing you already about this week's Truth, God Gives Us Life.

Read the Scripture verses for the week again and seek deeper understanding from God's Word.

Practice your memory verse.

What can you do to display a truer image of Jesus as you live your life every day?

Close in prayer.

DAY 5

Begin today's time with God by praying your memory verse back to God.

Read again all of the verses for Truth 2.

Dig a little deeper into God's Word and find other passages that teach you about how God Gives Us Life. List them here:

Close in prayer.

DAY 6

Week 2 is almost finished. I hope you have experienced God in ways you may have never known before. As you daily meet with God, He will bring a clearer and clearer understanding of why He Gives Us Life and the plans He has for you. While in prayer today, praise Him, thank Him again for the very breath you breathe, and ask Him to continue revealing His plans for your life. Pray for courage to be obedient and faithful in the everyday.

Review your memory verse.

List one or two ways you can apply the Truth: God Gives Us Life.

1.

2.

If your parents are alive, call them. Thank them for what they did to help you become who you are today. If you have children, be reminded again of the precious gift of life. Go hug them, tell them you love them, and share with them how much God loves them. Tell them how valuable their lives are to you and to God. Reach out to someone you know who is lonely, maybe feeling unloved or unappreciated, and reassure them of how much they mean to you, to others, and most importantly, to God.

DAY 7

If you are meeting with a small group as part of this study, use this day for your group meeting.

Here is a possible outline for your time together as a group:

Open Your Hearts:

- WORSHIP SONG: "Living Hope" — Phil Wickham

- PRAYER: Make this a time of silent prayer. Read Psalm 139:1-18 silently, offering the Scripture as a prayer of thanksgiving to God for creating and knowing us from the inside out!

- SCRIPTURE: Encourage one or two people to share the verse they memorized this week.

Discussion:

1. We all come from different backgrounds, family dynamics, geographic locations, and economic situations. God uses people from these diverse backgrounds for His glory. Share the conditions under which you were born.

2. Read Genesis 1:26-27. Why does God use the plural form, *"Let us make mankind in our image"*? (Refer to Job 33:4; Psalm 104:30; John 1:1-3; Colossians 1:15-17.)

3. What does it mean to be created in God's image?

4. Since we are created to be like Him, what characteristics should we display? Use the following Scriptures to help guide this discussion:

- Deuteronomy 32:4

- Isaiah 11:2-3

- Matthew 5:3-10, 44-45; 9:36

- Mark 10:45

- Luke 5:16; 23:34

- John 13:14-15

- Romans 9:15-16

- Philippians 2:6-8

- 1 John 4:7-8

5. How should "God Gives Us Life" and "*we are made in His image*" determine

- how we view God?

- how we view ourselves?

- how we view others?

Time of Commitment:

- WORSHIP SONG: "Who You Say I Am" — Hillsong Worship

- PRAYER: Encourage one or two people to offer a prayer of praise.

If you are not meeting with a small group, please take time on your own to go through the small group outline.

GOD GIVES US ABILITIES THAT GROW AND MATURE

I have a theory. If God were to say, "Okay, listen, you can have any ability you want. What do you want?", most people would say, "I want the ability to sing, and I'm not just talking about an ability. I'm talking about Grammy Award-winning ability!"

Singing. I've NEVER been good at it. In fact, I've been embarrassed by it. I get cold sweats any time I'm in a position where someone is going to hear me sing. Give me a ball to throw or catch, a bike to ride, or pretty much anything athletic, and I'm good.

My wife, Pam, is the exact opposite! She is a singer with degrees in vocal performance and music education, and has made a profession out of teaching others to sing. (Even my extremely gifted wife can't teach me to sing!)

Here's the point. God gives us different abilities and talents because He loves us and our world needs people with them. How boring it would be without the myriad of talents and abilities God has planted within the human race, which we see on display each day.

How should we react to this? Three things come to mind:

1. BETTER NEVER STOPS.

Never stop working to improve the talents and abilities that God has given you. Take lessons. Develop an ego that is healthy enough to learn from others who are better in that ability or talent. Pursue excellence, not perfection, and use the abilities and talents you have to glorify the One who gave them to you for His purposes.

2. RESPECT OTHERS.

Thanks to Pam's influence, I've learned to enjoy musical theater, concerts, and other musical performances far more as I've learned to respect the performers. I appreciate and respect the discipline, commitment, perseverance, and pure work ethic required to exercise any ability or talent with a high degree of professionalism and excellence.

3. THERE IS A PURPOSE.

God has a purpose for each of us. He's gifted us with the abilities and talents we need to accomplish His purposes. As I live life with Him every day, I learn more and more about the purpose for which He created me.

There is a wonderful story in Exodus 35-36, demonstrating this very point. The children of Israel were wandering in the Sinai Desert on their way from Egypt to the "promised land" that God had prepared for them. God instructed Moses to lead them to build a Tent of Meeting or tabernacle. This would be a portable, physical place where God would meet with His people. A sanctuary. A place of worship.

Notice how particular God was with His instructions. He didn't require or force anyone to give or donate their resources to support the project. He didn't force anyone to use their talents and abilities to complete the construction. Repeatedly, Moses wrote that those *"who were willing"* gave of their resources and their talents to fulfill God's desire for a tabernacle, a place to meet with His people.

It is also clear that God equipped His people with the specific resources, talents, and skills necessary. As each person was willing to give, as each person was willing to work, using the specific skills and talents He gave them, the tabernacle was completed.

As you read through the following passage from Exodus 35, look closely to see the amazing list of items God told Moses to have the skilled artisans make for the tabernacle. Circle each item and think about the skill sets required in an era without power tools, sewing machines, or the local hardware store. If God equipped these men and women to produce such items of beauty while wandering in the desert, just think how He has equipped you to do the tasks He has prepared for you.

Moses said to the whole Israelite community,... "All who are skilled among you are to come and make everything the LORD has commanded: the tabernacle with its tent and its covering, clasps, frames, crossbars, posts and bases; the ark with its poles and the atonement cover and the curtain that shields it; the table with its poles and all its articles and the bread of the Presence; the lampstand that is for light with its accessories, lamps and oil for the light; the altar of incense with its poles, the anointing oil and the fragrant incense; the curtain for the doorway at the entrance to the tabernacle; the altar of burnt offering with its bronze grating, its poles and all its utensils; the bronze basin with its stand; the curtains of the courtyard with its posts and bases, and the curtain for the entrance to the courtyard; the tent pegs for the tabernacle and for the courtyard, and their ropes; the woven garments worn for ministering in the sanctuary—both the sacred garments for Aaron the priest and the garments for his sons when they serve as priests."

Every skilled woman spun with her hands and brought what she had spun—blue, purple or scarlet yarn or fine linen. And all the women who were willing and had the skill spun the goat hair.

Then Moses said to the Israelites, "See, the LORD has chosen Bezalel son of Uri, the son of Hur, of the tribe of Judah, and he has filled him with the Spirit of God, with wisdom, with understanding, with knowledge and with all kinds of skills—to make artistic designs for work in gold, silver and bronze, to cut and set stones, to work in wood and to engage in all kinds of artistic crafts. And he has given both him and Oholiab son of Ahisamak, of the tribe of Dan, the ability to teach others. He has filled them with skill to do all kinds of work as engravers, designers, embroiderers in blue, purple and scarlet yarn and fine linen, and weavers—all of them skilled workers and designers." (Exodus 35:4, 10-19, 25-26, 30-35)

Wow! Do you think God knows what He wants? Did you notice the details? Interestingly, He not only knows what He wants, He knows who He wants us to become as we are obedient in using the talents and abilities that He has given to us.

In other words, as we use our talents and abilities for His purposes they grow and mature to the point at which we not only accomplish the specific task, but grow into who He needs us to be.

His purposes are accomplished through His people as we use the talents and abilities that He gives us, which continue to grow and mature throughout our lifetime.

Let this week be a time to explore how to live into the abilities and talents He's given you!

SCRIPTURE FOR TRUTH 3: GOD GIVES US ABILITIES THAT GROW AND MATURE

---

*Read these Scriptures and reflect upon how
God Gives Us Abilities that Grow and Mature.*

Then the LORD *said to Moses, "See, I have chosen Bezalel… and I have filled him with the Spirit of God, with wisdom, with understanding, with knowledge and with all kinds of skills— to make artistic designs for work in gold, silver and bronze, to cut and set stones, to work in wood, and to engage in all kinds of crafts. Moreover, I have appointed Oholiab… to help him. Also I have given ability to all the skilled workers to make everything I have commanded you."* — Exodus 31:1-6

And Jesus grew in wisdom and stature, and in favor with God and man.
— Luke 2:52

There he [Paul] met a Jew named Aquila, a native of Pontus, who had recently come from Italy with his wife Priscilla, because Claudius had ordered all Jews to leave Rome. Paul went to see them, and because he was a tentmaker as they were, he stayed and worked with them. Every Sabbath he reasoned in the synagogue, trying to persuade Jews and Greeks. — Acts 18:2-4

Just as a body, though one, has many parts, but all its many parts form one body, so it is with Christ. For we were all baptized by one Spirit so as to form one body—whether Jews or Gentiles, slave or free—and we were all given the one Spirit to drink. Even so the body is not made up of one part but of many. Now if the foot should say, "Because I am not a hand, I do not belong to the body," it would not for that reason stop being part of the body. And if the ear should say, "Because I am not an eye, I do not belong to the body," it would not for that reason stop being part of the body. If the whole body were an eye, where would the sense of hearing be? If the whole body were an ear, where would the sense of smell be? But in fact God has placed the parts in the body, every one of them, just as he wanted them to be — 1 Corinthians 12:12-18

PRAY – READ – APPLY – MEMORIZE – SHARE

-------------------- DAY 1 --------------------

Start your week off by offering praise and adoration to the Father, thanking Him for your talents and abilities. You might even ask Him to show you more clearly the talents and abilities He has entrusted to you. Ask God to reveal any unhealthy desires you may have had for a particular talent or ability, and ask for forgiveness. Pray for opportunities to develop and use *your* talents and abilities for Him from this day forward.

If you haven't already read through the introductory comments for Truth 3, read them now. Underline, highlight, or make notes in the margins as you read.

Read through the verses for Truth 3.

Close your time with God in prayer, thanking Him again for the talents and abilities with which He has gifted you.

-------------------- DAY 2 --------------------

Start your time with God in prayer.

Read aloud the verses and reflect upon how God Gives Us Abilities that Grow and Mature. Which verses resonate with you most? Identify a verse to memorize this week. Write it down here and begin memorizing it.

Answer these questions. Pray and think about how you can apply them to your life.

- If God said, "Pick an ability and I'll give it to you," what ability would you pick?

- Why does that ability sound interesting to you?

Close in prayer.

—————— **DAY 3** ——————

As you begin your time with God, ask the Holy Spirit to reveal what He wants you to learn.

Read the Scriptures and reflect upon how God Gives Us Abilities that Grow and Mature.

Rehearse your memory verse.

Answer these questions. Pray and think about how you can apply them to your life.

- What are the primary abilities and talents God has given you?

- What can you do to improve two or three of your abilities and talents?

Close in prayer.

——————— DAY 4 ———————

Begin with prayer, thanking God for what He is showing you already about this week's Truth, God Gives Us Abilities that Grow and Mature.

Read the Scripture verses for the week again and seek deeper understanding from God's Word.

Practice your memory verse.

Answer these questions. Pray and think about how you can apply them to your life.

- What abilities and talents do you see in the people closest to you?

- What can you do to encourage those closest to you in their abilities and talents?

- What do you think God is telling us by including a mention of the ability to teach others? (Exodus 35:34)

Close in prayer.

——————— **DAY 5** ———————

Begin today's time with God by praying your memory verse back to God.

Read again the verses for Truth 3.

Dig a little deeper into God's Word and find other passages that teach you about how God Gives Us Abilities that Grow and Mature. List them here:

Close in prayer.

——————— **DAY 6** ———————

Praise God for who He is, the Giver of all good and perfect things. Thank Him again for the talents and abilities He has given you and is developing within you.

Review your memory verse.

List one or two ways you can apply the Truth: God Gives Us Abilities that Grow and Mature.

   1.

   2.

Close in prayer.

——————— **DAY 7** ———————

If you are meeting with a small group as part of this study, use this day for your group meeting.

Here is a possible outline for your time together as a group:

Open Your Hearts:

- WORSHIP SONG: "Good Good Father" — Chris Tomlin
- PRAYER: Offer a prayer of thanksgiving.
- SCRIPTURE: Ask one or two people to share the verse they memorized this week.

Discussion:

1. If you could have ANY ability or talent, what would it be? Why?

2. Read Exodus 35:10-19. What skills did God give to the Israelites for the building of the tabernacle?

3. What other passages of Scripture did you find that teach how God Gives Us Abilities that Grow and Mature?

4. Name at least two abilities God has given you.

5. How can you use these abilities for Him?

6. What are some things you can do to grow in these abilities?

Time of Commitment:

- WORSHIP SONG: "How Great Thou Art" — Chris Rice
- PRAYER: Offer prayers of gratitude.

If you are not meeting with a small group, please take time on your own to go through the small group outline.

WE RECOGNIZE OUR SIN

S in.

It's ugly.

It's dark.

It's painful.

It haunts us.

It embarrasses us.

It breaks us.

It surrounds us.

It overwhelms us.

It highlights our weaknesses.

It destroys us from the inside out.

It hurts us.

It hurts those we love.

It hurts those who love us.

It hurts God.

It has consequences.

It's tempting.

It's temporarily pleasurable.

However, without the saving grace of Jesus, it condemns us to death and eternal separation from God.

Sin entered the world when Adam and Eve disobeyed God and chose to eat fruit from the "*tree of the knowledge of good and evil*" (Genesis 2:16-17; 3:1-24). A seemingly small decision—with the direst of consequences!

Bottom line, what is sin? It is disobedience to God.

My dad, Charles Wade, describes sin as "hurting anyone God loves. The hurt goes all the way to the Father's heart. The nature of sin is this: Loving things and using people rather than loving people and using things."

Are we all sinful? Yes. Can we help it? No. Are we born sinful? Yes. Does it have to define us? No.

I began to realize this truth at the age of six. As I think about it now, what kind of sin could I have committed at that young age that would cause me to worry? Frankly, I can't remember. All I knew was I loved Jesus, and I had disappointed Him. So, on a Sunday evening at Central Baptist Church in Italy, Texas, I went to the front of the church sanctuary where my dad, as the pastor, was standing. I told Daddy I wanted Jesus to save me from my sin, and I wanted Him to be Lord of my life.

While I couldn't have understood deep theological concepts at age six, I did know enough to realize that my sinful thoughts, actions, and habits were separating me from God. You may have had similar thoughts in the past, or you may be having them right now. Either way, we can be forgiven of our sin and live forever with Jesus:

> *No one will be declared righteous in God's sight by the works of the law; rather, through the law we become conscious of our sin.* (Romans 3:20)

> *For all have sinned and fall short of the glory of God.* (Romans 3:23)

> *But God demonstrates his own love for us in this: While we were still sinners, Christ died for us.* (Romans 5:8)

> *For the wages of sin is death, but the gift of God is eternal life in Christ Jesus our Lord.* (Romans 6:23)

> *For God so loved the world that he gave his one and only Son, that whoever believes in him shall not perish but have eternal life. For God did not send his Son into the world to condemn the world, but to save the world through him.* (John 3:16-17)

> *If you declare with your mouth, "Jesus is Lord," and believe in your heart that God raised him from the dead, you will be saved. For it is with your*

heart that you believe and are justified, and it is with your mouth that you profess your faith and are saved.... "Everyone who calls on the name of the Lord will be saved." (Romans 10:9-10, 13)

That Sunday evening, my dad helped me pray along the lines of: "Lord Jesus, I'm sorry for my sin. I know You are the Son of God. I know You died for my sin. I know You defeated sin when You arose from the grave. I want You to be Lord of my life and I want to follow You. I want to be obedient to You."

Even as a little boy in first grade, I felt a peace that comes when you know you've done the right thing.

But sin doesn't take a permanent vacation when a person prays for forgiveness and becomes a follower of Jesus. Fast forward nine years. I'm fifteen years old and in junior high school. During those years, let's just say my focus was not on Jesus and being obedient to Him. I was more worried about who my friends were and doing the things that were fun in the moment with them. It was not a healthy or thoughtful way to live, and I hid it well from my parents (or at least I think I did). But inside, I knew the decisions I was making were not right.

When I entered high school, I began to make some new friends. I joined the high school choir at our church—not because I enjoyed singing, but because they were going to Disney World during spring break. I had never been to Disney World, so choir was my ticket to the Magic Kingdom. The opportunity to go to Disney World outweighed my fear of singing!

That's when I began to "hang out" with a different crowd. The Holy Spirit began to convict me of the decisions I had been making. I rededicated my life to Jesus, saying again I wanted Him to be Lord of my life, and I wanted to live in a way that pleased Him.

Over the years, I have periodically felt the need to pause and rededicate myself to God's calling and His purposes. When that happens, it's typically a result of my selfish desires outweighing my obedience to His desires or a grateful heart giving way to a prideful one. At these times, I simply enter into His presence, ask Him to forgive me, and pray that the Holy Spirit will purify and permeate my heart. You will find, as I have, that God is faithful to forgive and restore.

Sin grips us. All of us. As children, teenagers, young adults, parents, and grandparents, we never escape sin in our lives. The great news is that we have a Savior. His name is Jesus.

Thank You, God, for loving us enough to send Jesus. Thank You, Jesus, for loving us enough to leave Heaven, live among us, and die for our sins. Thank You, God, for defeating sin, death, and the grave by raising Jesus to life and giving us access to life eternal with You through Him. Thank You, Holy Spirit, for working within us to purify our hearts and our minds, forming us into men and women after Your heart!

SCRIPTURE FOR TRUTH 4:
WE RECOGNIZE OUR SIN

---

*Read these Scriptures and reflect upon
how We Recognize Our Sin.*

Indeed, there is no one on earth who is righteous, no one who does what is right and never sins. — Ecclesiastes 7:20

We all, like sheep, have gone astray, each of us has turned to our own way; and the Lord has laid on him the iniquity of us all. — Isaiah 53:6

But who can discern their own errors? Forgive my hidden faults. Keep your servant also from willful sins; may they not rule over me. Then I will be blameless, innocent of great transgression. — Psalm 19:12-13

Therefore no one will be declared righteous in God's sight by the works of the law; rather, through the law we become conscious of our sin — Romans 3:20

...for all have sinned and fall short of the glory of God — Romans 3:23

Therefore, just as sin entered the world through one man, and death through sin, and in this way death came to all people, because all sinned — Romans 5:12

But God demonstrates his own love for us in this: While we were still sinners, Christ died for us. — Romans 5:8

For the wages of sin is death, but the gift of God is eternal life in Christ Jesus our Lord. — Romans 6:23

At one time we too were foolish, disobedient, deceived and enslaved by all kinds of passions and pleasures. We lived in malice and envy, being hated and hating one another. But when the kindness and love of God our Savior appeared, he saved us, not because of righteous things we had done, but because of his mercy. — Titus 3:3-5

PRAY – READ – APPLY – MEMORIZE – SHARE

———————— DAY 1 ————————

Begin with an offer of praise to the Father. Thank Jesus for His sacrificial, saving love. Pray the Holy Spirit will reveal insights as you read the Scriptures for Truth 4. If you have never asked Jesus to be your Savior and are ready to do so, take a moment to offer the same prayer my dad led me through. If you know Jesus, but your lifestyle isn't consistently aligning with His teachings, take a moment to admit it, ask for forgiveness, and seek His redeeming grace.

If you haven't already read through Truth 4's introductory comments, read them now. Underline, highlight, or make notes in the margins as you read.

Read through the verses for Truth 4.

Close your time with God in prayer, thanking Him for loving you in a way that keeps no record of wrongs.

———————— DAY 2 ————————

Start your time with God in prayer.

Read aloud the Scriptures and reflect upon how We Recognize Our Sin. Which verses resonate with you most? Identify a verse to memorize this week. Write it down here and begin memorizing it.

Whenever you are tempted to engage in a sinful action or thought, put God's Word to work in your life. Fire back with a memorized verse that you can repeat again and again until the temptation passes. The author of Psalm 119:11 teaches us this truth, *"I have hidden your word in my heart that I might not sin against you."* You will find great strength in memorizing God's Word and using it as a defense against sin.

Answer these questions. Pray and think about how you can make applications to your life.

- In what ways has sin caused harm to you?

- How is sin defining you now, or how has it defined you in the past?

- Have you asked Jesus to forgive you? If you haven't, what is holding you back?

As you close in prayer, take some time to sit quietly before God's throne and consider the magnitude of His salvation as He has erased the penalty of sin from your life. Respond to this realization with renewed gratitude.

——————— DAY 3 ———————

As you begin your time with God, ask the Holy Spirit to reveal what He wants you to learn.

Read the Scriptures and reflect upon how We Recognize Our Sin.

Rehearse your memory verse.

Answer these questions. Pray and think about how you can make applications to your life.

- In what ways has sin caused harm to your family?

- How do you feel when sin grips you or those you love?

- In what ways is the heart of God, the Father, hurt when we sin against ourselves or others?

Close in prayer, confessing sins that are present in your life. Ask God for forgiveness and the strength to stop willful sins that seem to control you. Intercede for the people who are important in your life. Pray God's strength in their lives to confess sin and live obediently. If they are not Christ's followers yet, pray they will be drawn to His love, forgiveness, and salvation.

—————— DAY 4 ——————

Begin with prayer, thanking God for what He is showing you already about this week's Truth, We Recognize Our Sin.

Read the verses for the week again and seek deeper understanding from God's Word.

Practice your memory verse.

Answer these questions. Pray and think about how you can make applications to your life.

- How do you stay accountable to living a life that pleases God?

- Who in your life helps you to stay accountable or could help you be more accountable?

- Who are you helping to hold accountable?

If a particular sin is gripping you to the point you feel powerless against it, find a spiritually mature Christian who has your best interest at heart. Ask them to pray for you. You may or may not know them well enough to reveal the actual sin, but you can ask them for prayer and an occasional follow-up, regarding your journey to break free of the sinful behavior.

As you close your time with prayer, thank God for the gift of godly friendships that help you stay accountable to holy living.

DAY 5

Begin today's time with God by praying your memory verse back to God.

Read again the verses for Truth 4.

Dig a little deeper into God's Word and find other passages that teach you about this week's Truth: We Recognize Our Sin. List Scriptures that teach you to acknowledge and recognize sin in your life.

Close in prayer, thanking God that His Word is living and powerful and that it helps you to clearly see the affect sin has on your relationship with Him.

—————— **DAY 6** ——————

Praise God for His saving power and thank Him for loving you enough to send Jesus.

Review your memory verse.

Being able to succinctly summarize your testimony is an important step in your journey with God. The basic concepts of your testimony can be pulled together by completing these simple statements:

- My life before I made Jesus my Lord can best be described as

- I realized I needed Jesus to forgive my sins when I understood that

- Now that I have chosen to follow Jesus as Lord and Savior, my life is

Close in prayer, thanking God again for His gift of salvation.

—————— DAY 7 ——————

If you are meeting with a small group as part of this study, use this day for your group meeting.

Here is a possible outline for your time together as a group:

Open Your Hearts

- WORSHIP SONG: "Flawless" — MercyMe

- PRAYER: Offer a prayer of praise.

- SCRIPTURE: Ask one or two people to share the verse they memorized this week.

Discussion

Read silently the Scriptures for Truth 4, then discuss the following questions:

1. What do these verses tell us about sin?

2. What other verses did you find this week that teach us about the Truth, We Recognize Our Sin?

3. In what ways does our sin harm us, our families, our friends, and our coworkers?

4. How do we stay accountable to living a life that pleases God?

5. Who in your life helps you stay accountable? Who are you helping to stay accountable?

6. If you have given your life to Christ, finish these sentences:

- My life before I made Jesus my Lord can best be described as…

- I realized I needed Jesus to forgive my sins when I understood that…

- Now that I have chosen to follow Jesus as Lord and Savior, my life is…

Time of Commitment

- WORSHIP SONG: "O Come to the Altar" — Elevation Worship

- Silent PRAYER: Follow the points below to guide your prayer:

  » Consider the magnitude of God's salvation as He has erased the penalty of sin from your life.

  » Thank Jesus for His great sacrifice for you.

  » If a particular sin is gripping you, ask God for forgiveness and healing.

  » Thank God for godly people who help keep you accountable.

  » Ask God to help you be obedient to Him.

  » If you have never asked Jesus to be your Savior and you are ready to do so, pray this prayer, "Lord Jesus, I'm sorry for my sin. I know You are the Son of God. I know You died for my sin. I know You defeated sin when You arose from the grave. I want You to be Lord of my life and I want to follow You. I want to be obedient to You." (If you prayed this prayer today, share your decision with your group.)

- PRAYER: Have one person close the prayer time with a prayer of praise and gratitude.

If you are not meeting with a small group, please take time on your own to go through the small group outline.

WE MEET JESUS

Who is Jesus? Why do we need to meet Him?

Jesus is the Son of God. "*As soon as Jesus was baptized, he went up out of the water. At that moment heaven was opened, and he saw the Spirit of God descending like a dove and alighting on him. And a voice from heaven said, 'This is my Son, whom I love; with him I am well pleased'*" (Matthew 3:16-17).

He is the Savior of the world. Jesus died in our place (Romans 5:8). We are all sinners, and He was the sacrifice for our sin (Romans 3:23; Hebrews 10:12-14). When He was raised from the dead (Romans 8:34), it proved He had victory over sin and can provide eternal life to anyone who receives Him (John 3:16-18, 36).

He is our coming King. The apostle Paul tells us in his letter to the church in Philippi, Greece, that one day "*every knee [will] bow, in heaven and on earth and under the earth, and every tongue acknowledge that Jesus Christ is Lord, to the glory of God the Father*" (Philippians 2:10-11).

He invites us to life with Him. The apostle John in Revelation 3:20 quotes Jesus as saying, "*Here I am! I stand at the door and knock. If anyone hears my voice and opens the door, I will come in and eat with that person, and they with me.*" This is a personal invitation to anyone who will receive it.

In *John Stott: The Making of a Leader*, Timothy Dudley-Smith references a reflection Dr. Stott offered on Revelation 3:20:

> Here, then, is the crucial question which we have been leading up to. Have we ever opened our door to Christ? Have we ever invited him in? This was exactly the question which I needed to have put to me. For, intellectually speaking, I had believed in Jesus all my life, on the other side of the door. I had regularly struggled to say my prayers through the key-hole. I had even pushed pennies under the door in a vain attempt to pacify him. I had been baptized, yes and confirmed as well. I went to church, read my Bible, had high ideals, and tried to be good and do good. But all the time, often without realising it, I was holding Christ at arm's length, and keeping him outside. I knew that to open the door might have momentous consequences. I am profoundly grateful to him for enabling me to open the door. Looking back now over more than fifty years, I realise that that simple step has changed the entire direction, course and quality of my life.[8]

Have you met Jesus? Have you opened the door to your heart where He is knocking? Have you opened it all the way or just cracked it a little? Have you opened it at one time, but now have pushed it closed again?

A few years ago, as we approached Christmas, a thought came to me early one Sunday morning: *Jesus is the answer. Now, what is the question?* Immediately, all these questions, which most of us have asked ourselves at some time or another, began to form in my mind. Do any of these sound familiar?

- Can I do this job?

- Can I pass this class?

- Can I accomplish my goals?

- Do I have the courage I need and am I really strong enough to overcome the challenges my career presents?

- Will I find favor in my work?

- Can I close the sales I need to close?

- Can I be successful in my career?

- Can I finish this degree?

- I'm financially in shambles. Will God really provide for my family?

- I've got all this junk going on in my life. Can I overcome the circumstances that I'm in?

- My marriage is a mess. Can we make it?

- My children are in trouble. They're not living the way they should. What do I do?

- I've got some important relationships that are in turmoil right now. How do I repair them?

- I know that Jesus loves me, but how does He love me?

- Does Jesus really love people like me?

- My child has died. How in the world do I keep going?

- Will I ever be truly happy, even joyful, after going through this divorce?

- How do I make it through the loss of my spouse?

- How do I survive the loss of my parent?

- Is Jesus really that powerful?

- Is our country going to be okay?

- What is the answer for a broken world?

No matter the question, Jesus is the answer! In essence, isn't that what God said when He sent Jesus? Isn't that what the writer of Hebrews was telling the early church? Isn't that what Paul preached and wrote? So, today, as we observe our world, the culture in which we live and the myriad of challenges, hurts, and joys that life brings our way, let me submit to you that Jesus is the answer. Now, what is *your* question?

Receive His invitation. Open the door to your heart.

SCRIPTURE FOR TRUTH 5:
WE MEET JESUS

---

*Read these Scriptures and reflect
upon how We Meet Jesus.*

---

*For to us a child is born, to us a son is given, and the government will
be on his shoulders. And he will be called Wonderful Counselor, Mighty
God, Everlasting Father, Prince of Peace. —* Isaiah 9:6

*For God so loved the world that he gave his one and only Son, that who-
ever believes in him shall not perish but have eternal life. For God did
not send his Son into the world to condemn the world, but to save the
world through him. —* John 3:16-17

*This is love: not that we loved God, but that he loved us and sent his Son
as an atoning sacrifice for our sins. —* 1 John 4:10

*In the beginning was the Word, and the Word was with God, and the
Word was God. He was with God in the beginning. Through him all
things were made; without him nothing was made that has been made.
—* John 1:1-3

*The Word became flesh and made his dwelling among us. We have seen
his glory, the glory of the one and only Son, who came from the Father,
full of grace and truth. —* John 1:14

*But when the set time had fully come, God sent his Son, born of a
woman, born under the law, to redeem those under the law, that we
might receive adoption to sonship. —* Galatians 4:4-5

*In the past God spoke to our ancestors through the prophets at many
times and in various ways, but in these last days he has spoken to us by his
Son, whom he appointed heir of all things, and through whom also he
made the universe. The Son is the radiance of God's glory and the exact
representation of his being, sustaining all things by his powerful word.
After he had provided purification for sins, he sat down at the right hand
of the Majesty in heaven. So, he became as much superior to the angels as
the name he has inherited is superior to theirs. —*Hebrews 1:1-4

The Son is the image of the invisible God, the firstborn over all creation. For in him all things were created: things in heaven and on earth, visible and invisible, whether thrones or powers or rulers or authorities; all things have been created through him and for him. He is before all things, and in him all things hold together. And he is the head of the body, the church; he is the beginning and the firstborn from among the dead, so that in everything he might have the supremacy. For God was pleased to have all his fullness dwell in him, and through him to reconcile to himself all things, whether things on earth or things in heaven, by making peace through his blood, shed on the cross. Once you were alienated from God and were enemies in your minds because of your evil behavior. But now he has reconciled you by Christ's physical body through death to present you holy in his sight, without blemish and free from accusation — Colossians 1:15-22*

For in Christ all the fullness of the Deity lives in bodily form — Colossians 2:9

Jesus answered, "I am the way and the truth and the life. No one comes to the Father except through me." — John 14:6

That at the name of Jesus every knee should bow, in heaven and on earth and under the earth, and every tongue acknowledge that Jesus Christ is Lord, to the glory of God the Father. — Philippians 2:10-12

PRAY – READ – APPLY – MEMORIZE – SHARE

——————— **DAY 1** ———————

Begin with an offer of praise to the Father. Thank Him for Jesus. Thank Him for loving you enough to send Jesus. Pray the Holy Spirit will reveal insights as you read the introductory comments and verses for this week.

If you haven't already read through Truth 5's introductory comments, read them now. Underline, highlight, or make notes in the margin as you read.

Read through the Scripture for Truth 5.

Close in prayer, thanking Jesus for loving you enough to leave Heaven, living on earth fully divine and fully human, then dying on the cross to offer you a way to live forever with Him in Heaven.

——————— **DAY 2** ———————

Begin your time with God in prayer.

Read aloud the Scriptures for Truth 5 and reflect upon how We Meet Jesus. Which verses resonate with you most? Identify a verse to memorize this week. Write it down here and begin memorizing it.

Answer these questions. Pray and think about how you can make application to your life.

- Have you met Jesus?

- If someone asked, "What does Jesus mean to you?" how would you answer?

- Is Jesus the Lord of your life? What segments of your life do you need to let go of and let Him have control?

Close your daily time with God in prayer, expressing your love for your Savior.

———————— DAY 3 ————————

Begin your time with God with praise and by asking the Holy Spirit to reveal what He wants you to learn about this week's Truth, We Meet Jesus, as you read the Scriptures again for this week.

Rehearse your memory verse.

Answer these questions. Pray and think about how you can make application to your life.

- Look back toward the beginning of Truth 5, find the quote from *John Stott: The Making of a Leader*. In what ways do you relate to Dr. Stott's observations?

- Reflect on Dr. Stott's final sentence: "I realise that that simple step has changed the entire direction, course and quality of my life." How has the "simple step" (of opening the door of your heart and making Jesus your Lord) changed the direction, course, and quality of your life?

Close in prayer, thanking God for changing the course of your life through His Son, Jesus Christ.

—————— DAY 4 ——————

Begin with prayer, thanking God for what He is showing you already about this week's Truth, We Meet Jesus.

Read the Scriptures for the week again and ask God to open your eyes and your heart to His Word.

Practice your memory verse.

Answer these questions. Pray and think about how you can make application to your life.

- Refer to the long list of questions at the end of this week's introductory comments. What are the three biggest questions you are asking yourself right now? (If needed, add questions that target your biggest concerns.)

- How is Jesus the answer to those questions?

- Which of the Scripture references for Truth 5 support the idea that Jesus is the answer to your questions? List them here.

Wrap up your time with God by praising Him for being the answer to all of life's questions.

DAY 5

Begin today's time with God by praying your memory verse back to God.

Read again the verses for Truth 5.

Dig a little deeper into God's Word and find other passages that teach you about how We Meet Jesus. What other Scriptures introduce you to Jesus? List them here.

Look at Matthew, chapters 8-9, and list the people who met Jesus. From your list, identify the ones whose lives were forever changed. Then identify those who experienced no apparent change. What caused the difference?

Close in prayer, thanking God for the change that came into your life when you met Jesus.

—————— **DAY 6** ——————

Start your time with God with praise for how He has blessed your life since you met Jesus.

Read back through the Scriptures for this week, giving special focus to Colossians 1:15-22. Let the majesty and beauty of this passage sink deep into your heart.

Review your memory verse.

Think of someone you already know, and commit to tell them what Jesus has done in your life lately. List at least three examples of His work in your life now.

Ask God to give you an opportunity to share a word of encouragement with someone else who needs to hear that Jesus loves them. How can you help someone else meet Jesus?

Close your time in prayer, speaking Colossians 1:15-22 back to the Lord as a direct praise, as well as a confession of faith. (Example: You are the image of the invisible God, the firstborn over all creation. For in You all things were created: things in heaven and on earth, visible and invisible, whether thrones or powers or rulers or authorities; all things have been created through You and for You....)

DAY 7

If you are meeting with a small group as part of this study, use this day for your group meeting.

Here is a possible outline for your time together as a group:

Open Your Hearts

- WORSHIP SONG: "Jesus Paid It All" — Shane & Shane

- PRAYER: Ask one or two people to offer a prayer of gratitude.

- SCRIPTURE: Encourage one or two people to share the verse they memorized this week.

Discussion

Read aloud the Scriptures for We Meet Jesus.

1. If you were asked the question, "What does Jesus mean to you?", how would you answer?

2. What does it mean for Jesus to be Lord of your life?

3. Read the reflection by Dr. Stott in the commentary for Truth 5. In what ways do you relate?

4. Re-read the last sentence of the reflection. Discuss how the "simple step" changed the direction, course, and quality of your life.

5. Refer to the long lists of questions at the end of this week's commentary. What are the three biggest questions you are asking yourself right now? What other questions would you add to the list?

6. How is Jesus the answer to those questions? Which of the Scriptures for Truth 5 support this?

7. Read Colossians 1:15-22 again. Share three examples of God's work in your life right now.

Time of Commitment:

- WORSHIP SONG: "In Christ Alone" — Shane & Shane
- PRAYER:
  - » Speak Colossians 1:15-22 silently back to the Lord. (Example: You are the image of the invisible God, the firstborn over all creation. For in You all things were created:...)
  - » Ask one or two people to close the group time with prayer.

If you are not meeting with a small group, please take time on your own to go through the small group outline.

WE CHOOSE JESUS

What is life like in Hell? I don't know. It must be utterly devastating, painful, horrific, and hopeless. Frankly, there are no words to adequately describe eternal separation from God. How do we know this to be true? Jesus never would have come to earth as a human and died on a cross if eternity in Hell, separated forever from God, is just a little uncomfortable.

Yet, God—in His Sovereignty, with all He invested in saving us from a life separated from Him—still allows us to choose: believe in Jesus and receive Him, or don't believe and reject Him. Why is this a choice and not a command? Let me ask you this question: Can you have a healthy relationship with anyone without choice?

Healthy relationships are the fruit of *choice, communication,* and *commitment.* When I was seventeen years old, I *chose* to ask my friend, Pam Childers, out on a "real date." We *communicated* that evening over pizza and a stroll through the colorful Fort Worth Water Gardens. Our *commitment* to each other deepened a little. I followed the advice of my dad: "Son, if you have a good time on a date, book the next date before you drop her off at her house." I chose to schedule the next date, and fortunately for me, she said yes!

Over the following five years, through the end of high school and our college years at Baylor University, we continued this pattern of *choosing* each other, *communicating* with each other, and deepening our *commitment* to each other. Today, even after thirty-six years of marriage, this pattern of *choice, communication,* and *commitment* continues.

Interestingly, when one of us *chooses* poorly, our *communication* suffers and our *commitment* lessens. When our *communication* is spotty, our *commitment* is not what it should be and we make unfortunate *choices*. At times, when our *commitment* is not on the level it should be, we *choose* unwisely and our *communication* drops to nonexistent.

Choice, communication, and *commitment* form a cycle that leads to either a healthy or unhealthy relationship. You may be thinking, *Really, can it be summed up that succinctly?*

Yes. Think about it—we make *choices* all day, every day. From the moment we awake until the moment we go to sleep, our life is one *choice* after another. Will I eat a salad or a hamburger? Will I workout or watch TV? Will I take responsibility or shuffle it off on another? Will I do what I know to be right, or will I cave to external pressures? Will I encourage myself and others or cut us all down? Will I *choose* a positive attitude or a negative one? Will I share my feelings or keep them bottled inside? Will I listen or ignore? Will I spend time with God or with another?

You make *choices* all day, every day. And there are always relational consequences, good and bad, depending upon, yes, your *choices*!

Communication—is it more about talking or listening? It depends. Part of wisdom is knowing when to talk and when to listen.

The Bible has much to say about our talk (124 references), our tongue (133 references), the way we speak (450 references), and our speech (39 references).[9] God cares about *what* we say and the *way* we say it. Jesus' brother, James, wrote, "*With the tongue we praise our Lord and Father, and with it we curse human beings, who have been made in God's likeness*" (James 3:9). Why? Because our speech reflects the condition of our hearts.

As the Holy Spirit permeates your heart, the fruit of His Spirit becomes more evident in many ways, not the least of which is your speech. The way you talk to others demonstrates love, joy, peace, patience, kindness, goodness, faithfulness, gentleness, and self-control (Galatians 5:22-23 ESV). As this fruit is more consistent and evident in your speech, it improves your relationships. People will not always remember what you say; they will remember how you make them feel when you say it.

At the same time, great *communication* is so much more than talking. The Bible also has plenty to say about listening (in the *New International Version*, 412 references for *listen* and 22 for *listening*).[10] We all have a deep human need to be heard. When you listen, sincerely listen, to another person, you are saying:

- You are important to me.

- I value your opinion.

- I care more about what you have to say than what I have to say.

- I want to hear you and understand you.

Listening to understand another person unlocks the door to their heart. It is the key to an appropriate amount of intimacy in every relationship. You don't lose intimacy in relationships by not talking; you lose it by *choosing* not to listen.[11]

Your *choices* related to the way you *communicate* have a profound impact on the health of your relationships!

As you make *choices* and as you *communicate*, the level of *commitment* in a relationship is impacted. You've seen it. You've experienced it. You *commit* to what is important and to those who are important to you. When others *choose* you and effectively *communicate* with you, you feel a deeper *commitment* to them, and they feel it toward you.

The more *committed* two people are, the easier it is to *choose* one another over other things and other people. Then, as we *choose* well, *communication* flows more clearly, and we deepen the level of *commitment* even further.

This week, let's consider how *choice, communication,* and *commitment* drive your spiritual relationship with the Creator. Think about your relationship with Jesus. Would you characterize it as healthy or unhealthy? Growing or stagnant? Authentic or superficial? What word would you use to describe the kind of relationship you want to have with God?

For a long time, when asked what kind of relationship that I wanted with God, I would answer with the word *authentic*. Authentic is a great word. It speaks to character, integrity, intent, wholeness, and who we are when no one is looking. It is a comforting way to describe any relationship. Over the last few years, however, my word for describing the type of relationship I want with God has changed. The word is now *healthy*. As we age, as we watch our parents grow older, *healthy* becomes a more important word.

How do we have a healthy relationship with God? Simply stated, we *choose* Him. We *communicate* with Him. We *commit* our lives to Him. As we live life every day, we are continually faced with *choice, communication,* and *commitment.* How will we live these out?

The most important decision you and I will ever make is whether we will choose Jesus to be the Lord of our lives, or choose something else, anything else to be lord of our lives. The consequences of this one decision outweigh any other decision we ever make, not just for life in the everyday, but for life in the eternal.

When we choose Jesus as Savior, the consequences are indescribably amazing, as Paul told the Ephesians, "*Now to him who is able to do immeasurably more than all we can ask or even imagine*" (Ephesians 3:20).

But the consequences of rejecting Jesus as Savior are indescribably devastating. To refuse to accept His gift of forgiveness means you must bear the weight of your sin alone. The Bible is clear on what that leads to—eternal separation from God's holy presence (John 3:18, 36).

In summary, God desperately wants a healthy relationship with every human being. If He didn't, He never would have sent Jesus, and Jesus never would have chosen to come to earth fully human and, at the same time, fully divine as the ransom for our sins. Yet, God loves us too much to force Himself upon us.

Will you choose Jesus? When you do, you are privileged to live life with Him every day. And to help you, His Spirit will abide with you.

So, what will it be? Will you *choose* Jesus? He invites you to *choose* well.

SCRIPTURE FOR TRUTH 6:
WE CHOOSE JESUS

Read these Scriptures and reflect
upon how We Choose Jesus.

Come to me, all you who are weary and burdened, and I will give you rest. Take my yoke upon you and learn from me, for I am gentle and humble in heart, and you will find rest for your souls. For my yoke is easy and my burden is light. — Matthew 11:28-30

"Come, follow me," Jesus said, "and I will send you out to fish for people." — Matthew 4:19

Whoever wants to be my disciple must deny themselves and take up their cross and follow me. — Matthew 16:24

If you want to be perfect [complete], *go, sell your possessions and give to the poor, and you will have treasure in heaven. Then come, follow me.* — Matthew 19:21

I am the light of the world. Whoever follows me will never walk in darkness, but will have the light of life. — John 8:12

Therefore, do not let sin reign in your mortal body so that you obey its evil desires. — Romans 6:12

My sheep listen to my voice; I know them, and they follow me. — John 10:27

Whoever believes in him is not condemned, but whoever does not believe stands condemned already because they have not believed in the name of God's one and only Son — John 3:18

Whoever believes in the Son has eternal life, but whoever rejects the Son will not see life, for God's wrath remains on them. — John 3:36

Yet to all who did receive him, to those who believed in his name, he gave the right to become children of God—children born not of natural descent, nor of human decision or a husband's will, but born of God. — John 1:12-13

Here I am! I stand at the door and knock. If anyone hears my voice and opens the door, I will come in and eat with that person, and they with me. — Revelation 3:20

PRAY – READ – APPLY – MEMORIZE – SHARE

—————— DAY 1 ——————

After offering a word of praise and thanksgiving to the Father, tell Jesus you *choose* Him. Ask the Holy Spirit to help you build a healthy relationship with Him as you *choose* Him, *communicate* with Him, and deepen your *commitment* to Him and to His purposes.

If you haven't already read through the introductory comments for Truth 6, read them now. Underline, highlight, or make notes in the margin as you read.

Read through the Scriptures for Truth 6.

Close in prayer with a heart full of thanks that God wants to have an ongoing, healthy relationship with you.

—————— DAY 2 ——————

Begin your time with God in prayer.

Read aloud the Scriptures for Truth 6 and reflect upon how We Choose Jesus. Which verses resonate with you most? Identify a verse to memorize this week. Write it down here and begin memorizing it.

Answer these questions. Pray and think about how you can apply them to your life.

- If someone asked you, "Why should I choose Jesus? Why is a relationship with Jesus important?", what would you say?

- Have you chosen Jesus? If so, how did your life begin to change after choosing Him?

- If you have not chosen Jesus yet, will you choose Him now? Why?

Close your daily time with God in prayer, expressing to Him why you have chosen to follow Him.

DAY 3

Today, as you begin your time with God, ask the Holy Spirit to reveal what He wants you to learn about how We Choose Jesus as you read the Scriptures again for this week.

Rehearse your memory verse.

Answer these questions. Pray and think about how you can make application in your life.

- What word have you used in the past to describe the kind of relationship you *wanted* with Jesus?

- What word describes the kind of relationship you have with Him *right now*?

- What word describes the kind of relationship you *would like* to have with Jesus?

Close with prayer.

DAY 4

Begin with prayer, thanking God for what He is showing you already about this week's Truth, We Choose Jesus.

Read the Scriptures for the week again, marking those that speak most deeply to your heart.

Practice your memory verse.

What three things can you do, in the everyday, to grow a healthy relationship with Jesus?

Close by praying back to God several of the verses you marked in today's study time.

DAY 5

Begin today's time with God by praying your memory verse back to God.

Read again the verses for Truth 6.

Dig a little deeper into God's Word and find other passages that teach you about how We Choose Jesus. List them here:

Close in prayer, thanking God for opening your eyes to new insights in His Word.

DAY 6

Open your time with God by praising Him.

Review your memory verse.

Think about a relationship you have that moved from unhealthy to healthy. Identify how *choice, communication,* and *commitment* led to creating this healthy relationship. Write a brief summary of this transition below.

A perfect example may be how you came to *choose* Jesus. Describe how and when you made that choice.

Read the Scriptures for Truth 6 again.

List one or two ways, times, or experiences in which you can apply the Truth: We Choose Jesus.

1.

2.

Close with a prayer of gratitude to God.

DAY 7

If you are meeting with a small group as part of this study, use this day for your group meeting.

Here is a possible outline for your time together as a group:

Open Your Hearts

- WORSHIP SONG: "Jesus I Believe" — Big Daddy Weave

- PRAYER: Encourage one or two people to offer a prayer of commitment.

- SCRIPTURE: Ask one or two people to share the verse they memorized this week.

Discussion

1. If someone asked, "Why should I choose Jesus?", what would be your answer?

2. What word best describes the kind of relationship you would like to have with Jesus?

3. Read aloud the Scriptures for Truth 6. What is the "choice" in each one?

4. On Day 6, you were asked to think about a relationship that moved from unhealthy to healthy. Identify how *choice, communication,* and *commitment* led to creating this healthy relationship. Share with the group.

5. What are three things you can do to grow a healthy relationship with Jesus?

6. Discuss one or two ways you can apply the truth, We Choose Jesus, in your everyday life.

Time of Commitment

- WORSHIP SONG: "Give Me Jesus" — Danny Gokey
- PRAYER: Close the group time with prayer.

If you are not meeting with a small group, please take time on your own to go through the small group outline.

WE RECEIVE
THE HOLY SPIRIT

Have you ever been in a situation, job, marriage, college class, or doctoral program where you knew you needed help? Where, without a doubt, you were "in over your head"? You constantly had this feeling of anxiety, being in a state of turmoil seemingly without end? You came to the realization that "I can't do this in my own power"?

This was exactly the place I found myself in, when I began a sales career in straight commission sales. After fourteen years of financial analysis and planning (and the predictable income), I left it to pursue a career in outside sales.

Quickly, I realized, "I can't do this in my own power." Frequently, I would be filled with anxious thoughts about making enough sales. *Am I going to be able to provide for my family? What if no one buys from me today? Am I good enough to do this?* You get the picture.

Having been raised in a Christian home with parents who consistently modeled dependence on the Lord, along with the experience Pam and I already had in trusting Him, this anxiety caused me to seek the Lord in prayer every morning in a way I had never experienced before.

Ashamedly, at thirty-six years old, I had not once been through a season of life where I had consistent, daily time with the Lord. It all changed in the late summer and early fall of 1998. As I began my sales career, the cold reality set in that if I made sales, my family would eat, and if I didn't, we wouldn't. This reality drove me to the Lord.

Early every morning, I would be on my knees in my dining room, praying—praising His name and seeking His presence, His wisdom, His courage, His provision. I began reading a 365-day chronological Bible. When reading the Old Testament, one of my favorite sections in the chronological Bible is in the book of 1 Samuel. While reading Samuel's writings about David running for his life from King Saul, I also read the psalms that David wrote while in the midst of running, hiding, and trying to stay alive.

In reading those psalms, I heard David's heart. I could *feel* his heart—the anxiety, the fear, the very real dependence on God in the everyday! Not knowing what that day, or the next, or the next would hold, just knowing and taking refuge in the fact that God was his provider, his sustainer, his protector for that particular day. It overwhelmed me, and I took great comfort in God's desire to hold me, provide for me, direct me, and care for my family.

I read in Exodus 3:21 where Moses wrote, "*And I* [God] *will make the Egyptians favorably disposed toward this people, so that when you leave you will not go empty-handed.*" In my own time with God, I began to pray that God would favorably dispose the hearts of the people I would be seeing that day and that He would give me a pure heart, that my motives would be pure, that I would be "on the give and not on the take."

One morning, I read 1 Kings 17. It's the story of Elijah and the widow. There was a drought in Israel. Elijah, God's prophet, was directed by God to go see a widow who would provide food for him. When he met the widow, she was gathering sticks to build a fire and prepare a meal for herself and her son. As she explained to Elijah, it would be their final meal. She only had a small amount of flour and oil, so she would make this meal, they would eat it, and then they would die.

Boldly and obediently, Elijah instructed her to make a loaf of bread for him and then prepare one for herself and her son. As Elijah explained in 1 Kings 17:14-16:

> For this is what the LORD, the God of Israel, says: "The jar of flour will not be used up and the jug of oil will not run dry until the day the LORD sends rain on the land." She went away and did as Elijah had told her. So, there was food every day for Elijah and for the woman and her family. For the jar of flour was not used up and the jug of oil did not run dry, in keeping with the word of the LORD spoken by Elijah.

I'll never forget the insight the Holy Spirit gave me that morning. He revealed to me that the jar of flour and the jug of oil were not filled up to the brim so that the widow and Elijah could physically see there was plenty of provision for that day and the next. Instead, there was just enough for each day.

I took the Scripture at face value and trusted what God was showing me: when we are obedient to His calling (as Elijah and the widow were, and as I was trying to be), then we can trust God in the everyday to provide every day.

I read 2 Chronicles 31:21 where Ezra wrote about King Hezekiah: "*In everything that he undertook in the service of God's temple and in obedience to the law and the commands, he sought his God and worked wholeheartedly. And so he prospered.*"

Again, I took God's Word at face value and trusted it. This Scripture became my "formula for success." Seek God in prayer and Scripture, work wholeheartedly with everything that was in me, and then trust Him to provide. It was up to God how He wanted to "prosper" me. My job was simply to seek Him, then go do the work—wholeheartedly—to the best of my ability in His power, not my own.

Most of us have heard the old saying, "Pray like it all depends on God and work like it all depends on me." That morning, when I read 2 Chronicles 31:21, the reality set in that if I would seek Him through prayer and Scripture and work wholeheartedly with everything that was in me, I could trust His provision. I didn't have to do my work in my own power. His Spirit would lead me. His power would be present and on display in my life.

In Ephesians 3:20-21, Paul prayed, "*Now to him who is able to do immeasurably more than all we ask or imagine, according to his power that is at work within us, to him be glory in the church and in Christ Jesus throughout all generations, for ever and ever! Amen.*" Again, I took God's Word at face value and trusted it. I began to pray that He would provide immeasurably more than all I could ask or imagine because of His power at work in me—not because of my power but His, and not for my glory but for His glory. I didn't want the credit. It wasn't mine to have. God was at work in me and through me to accomplish His purposes by the power of the Holy Spirit.

These Scriptures and others led me on this journey to more fully realize that the Holy Spirit was at work in me. I began praying that the Holy Spirit would permeate my being and take over my heart, my mind, and my life. I prayed that

He would polish out all the cracks in my heart caused by sin and that I would reflect a truer image of God. My prayer was that in every encounter I had with others, they would see Jesus in me.

SCRIPTURE FOR TRUTH 7: WE RECEIVE THE HOLY SPIRIT

---

*Read these Scriptures and reflect upon
how We Receive the Holy Spirit.*

---

*If you love me, keep my commands. And I will ask the Father, and he
will give you another advocate to help you and be with you forever—
the Spirit of truth. The world cannot accept him, because it neither sees
him nor knows him. But you know him, for he lives with you and will
be in you.* —John 14:15-17

*Anyone who loves me will obey my teaching. My Father will love them,
and we will come to them and make our home with them.* — John
14:23

*But the Advocate, the Holy Spirit, whom the Father will send in my
name, will teach you all things and will remind you of everything I have
said to you.* — John 14:26

*On one occasion, while he was eating with them, he gave them this com-
mand: "Do not leave Jerusalem, but wait for the gift my Father promised, which you have heard me speak about. For John baptized with
water, but in a few days you will be baptized with the Holy Spirit."*
— Acts 1:4-5

*Peter replied, "Repent and be baptized, every one of you, in the name of
Jesus Christ for the forgiveness of your sins. And you will receive the gift
of the Holy Spirit."* — Acts 2:38

*After they prayed, the place where they were meeting was shaken. And
they were all filled with the Holy Spirit and spoke the word of God
boldly.* — Acts 4:31

*We are witnesses of these things, and so is the Holy Spirit, whom God has
given to those who obey him.* — Acts 5:32

*While Peter was still speaking these words, the Holy Spirit came on all
who heard the message. The circumcised believers who had come with
Peter were astonished that the gift of the Holy Spirit had been poured
out even on Gentiles.* — Acts 10:44-45

May the God of hope fill you with all joy and peace as you trust in him, so that you may overflow with hope by the power of the Holy Spirit. — Romans 15:13

Do you not know that your bodies are temples of the Holy Spirit, who is in you, whom you have received from God? You are not your own; — 1 Corinthians 6:19

Because you are his sons, God sent the Spirit of his Son into our hearts, the Spirit who calls out, "Abba, Father." — Galatians 4:6

And you also were included in Christ when you heard the message of truth, the gospel of your salvation. When you believed, you were marked in him with a seal, the promised Holy Spirit — Ephesians 1:13

Now to him who is able to do immeasurably more than all we ask or imagine, according to his power that is at work within us, to him be glory in the church and in Christ Jesus throughout all generations, for ever and ever! Amen. — Ephesians 3:20-21

PRAY – READ – APPLY – MEMORIZE – SHARE

──────── DAY 1 ────────

Start your time with God by praising Him for who He is, the Author and Perfecter of our faith, the Giver of all good and perfect things. Thank Him for the indwelling of His Spirit. Thank Him for the hope you have by the power of His Spirit. Ask the Holy Spirit to permeate your heart and your mind. Ask Him to give you wisdom in the moment to listen, to know what to say and what not to say.

If you haven't already read through the introductory comments for Truth 7, read them now. Underline, highlight, or make notes in the margin as you read.

Read through the Scriptures for Truth 7.

Close in prayer, asking God to lead you as you go about this very day and to trust Him to do so.

──────── DAY 2 ────────

Start your time with God by thanking Him that He makes the Holy Spirit available to you, so you are never alone, never without the Lord Himself.

Read aloud the Scriptures for Truth 7 and reflect upon how We Receive the Holy Spirit. Which verses resonate with you the most? Identify a verse to memorize this week. Write it down here and begin memorizing it.

Answer these questions. Pray and think about how you can make them apply to your life.

- In what areas of your life are you anxious?

- In what ways are you trying to live life in your own power?

- What parts of your life need to be turned over to Him?

As you close your daily time with God in prayer, begin to relinquish the parts of your life that you have been holding onto too tightly.

—————— DAY 3 ——————

Begin by praying for the Holy Spirit to open the eyes of your heart to the deep truths He has for you today as you explore how We Receive the Holy Spirit more completely.

Read again the Scriptures for this week.

Rehearse your memory verse.

Answer these questions. Pray and think about how you can make them apply to your life.

- What would be different if you sought God every day?

- What would be different if you worked wholeheartedly?

Close with prayer, making a commitment to seek God with your whole heart today.

DAY 4

Begin with prayer, thanking God for what He is showing you already about this week's Truth, We Receive the Holy Spirit.

Read the Scriptures for the week again and underline all that we receive as gifts from the Holy Spirit.

Practice your memory verse.

Answer these questions. Pray and think about how you can make them apply to your life.

- What would be different if you trusted Him to do "immeasurably more"?

- How have you seen "immeasurably more" already in your life?

Close by praying back to God one or more verses that have been especially meaningful for you this week.

—————— **DAY 5** ——————

Begin today's time with God by praying your memory verse back to Him.

Read again the verses for Truth 7.

Dig a little deeper into God's Word and find other passages that teach you about how We Receive the Holy Spirit. What Scriptures do you find that introduce you to the Holy Spirit? List them here:

Close in prayer, thanking God for His ever present Spirit, who comforts and corrects us.

—————— **DAY 6** ——————

Open your time with God by praising Him.

Review your memory verse.

Think of a time in your life when you felt "in over your head." As you look back on that experience, how was the Holy Spirit—His power, His hope—at work in your life?

Read the Scriptures for Truth 7 again.

List one or two ways, times, or experiences in which you can apply the Truth: We Receive the Holy Spirit.

1.

2.

Close with a prayer of gratitude to God .

 **DAY 7**

If you are meeting with a small group as part of this study, use this day for your group meeting.

Here is a possible outline for your time together as a group:

Open Your Hearts

- WORSHIP SONG: "Holy Spirit" — Francesca Battistelli

- PRAYER: Offer prayers of commitment.

- SCRIPTURE: Encourage one or two people to share the verse they memorized this week.

Discussion

1. In what areas of your life are you anxious? In what ways are you trying to live life in your own power? What do you need to turn over to God?

2. What would be different if you sought God in these areas every day?

3. Tell about a time in your life when you experienced immeasurably more.

4. How does a spirit of entitlement versus an attitude of gratitude affect your view of immeasurably more?

5. On Day 3, you were asked to read the Scriptures and underline all of the gifts we receive from the Holy Spirit. What are these gifts?

6. Share your experience from Day 6 about a time when the Holy Spirit was at work in your life.

Time of Commitment

- WORSHIP SONG: "Spirit of the Living God" — Vertical Worship
- PRAYER: Ask one or two people to offer a prayer of surrender.

If you are not meeting with a small group, please take time on your own to go through the small group outline.

WE RECEIVE
SPIRITUAL GIFTS

When it comes to gifts, do you enjoy giving or receiving more? Trick question? Maybe, but I think it's a fair question. In my life, whether I have enjoyed giving or receiving more depended on my stage of life.

When I was eleven years old, I asked for a ten-speed bicycle for Christmas. Why? I had plenty of sound, logical reasons. First, ten-speed bicycles were "cool." (In other words, I would be cool riding it.) Second, it wasn't a kid's bike. I considered it a "big boy bike," unlike the one I felt I had outgrown. And third, it would be useful for my job. I delivered newspapers every morning in our neighborhood using my bike as the primary means of transportation.

Even with these very practical and compelling reasons, I still wasn't sure if my parents would give me a ten-speed. The ten-speed was a new invention back in the early 1970s, having just been introduced to the market. They were expensive and unknown, but neither of these concerns created a reasonable argument, at least in my mind, to justify not giving me a ten-speed!

As we approached Christmas that year, I utilized all the sales skills I knew at that time to persuade my parents. Even with the immense sales ability I felt I possessed as an eleven-year-old boy, the reality of receiving a ten-speed was "up in the air."

Like many families, we alternated sharing Christmas Day with my grandparents. One year we would be with my mom's parents and the next with my dad's parents. This particular year, we were to be with my mom's parents in the thriving metropolis of Frederick, Oklahoma.

I'll never forget that trip to my grandparents' home. We left our house in the late afternoon on Christmas Eve. All six of us were packed into the front two rows of seats in the family station wagon. Of course, there were no seatbelt laws at that time, so we sat three across in the front seat and three across in the back seat. My parents had folded down the third row and packed all of our luggage and all of the Christmas presents in the back portion of "the wagon." Then they covered everything with layers of blankets, so my three sisters and I couldn't see our presents. I was still in the dark on whether a ten-speed was in the cards for me.

Two of my sisters and I sat in the back seat. We had strict instructions from my mom to keep all arms and legs in front of us—no turning around and trying to touch or see any of the presents! As we traveled and nightfall came, it got very dark in the car. That was the moment I was waiting for. I had already bribed one of my sisters to reach her hand over the back of our seat and try to feel under the blankets for a tire or a handlebar or anything that would confirm that a bicycle was hidden there. While she did that, I provided "cover" by leaning forward to engage my parents in conversation.

As the miles sped by on that dark winter evening, I waited, heart beating fast, mind spinning with hope, until my sister gave me the results of her clandestine investigation. Sure enough, she felt a tire! It was connected to a ten-speed bike. At that moment, life for me was great.

Receiving wonderful gifts is fun.

Fast forward about sixteen years and our oldest son, Caleb, was eighteen months old. He couldn't tell us what he wanted for Christmas, so Pam and I took him to Toys"R"Us, turned him loose, and followed him to see what captivated his attention. Not long into our shopping excursion, he found that Little Tikes red car with the yellow top. It had a door that opened, a seat to sit in, a steering wheel to grab, and a foot-powered "Fred Flintstone" motor. He drove himself all over the store and had a great time. We knew we had the perfect gift for him!

As you might imagine, it wasn't very pleasant pulling him out of that little car in the middle of Toys"R"Us. But on Christmas morning, when I carried him down the stairs and he saw that car again, his face beamed, his smile went ear to ear, and he screamed with excitement. We did it! We gave him "the perfect gift." Pam and I felt great about it!

Giving wonderful gifts is fun.

In a small way, this is a similar feeling to what our Father in Heaven has as He gives the perfect spiritual gifts to each of us. Imagine our Heavenly Father's joy when we choose Jesus, the perfect gift from Heaven who saves us from our sin. Imagine His sheer delight when He is then able to give us the perfect spiritual gifts that He knows we need to fulfill the purposes to which He has called us.

Giving gifts is a big part of who God is. After all, as both Matthew and James have written, God is the Father who gives good and perfect gifts (Matthew 7:11; James 1:17). Think about some of the gifts God gives us. What about rest? It's a gift from God. Parents, children, friends, sunrises, sunsets, vacations, food, water, breath—the list could go on and on. God loves us, He created us in His image, so He showers us with gifts of all kinds!

God also gives us spiritual gifts, according to Paul and the writer of Hebrews. They are not random. We don't draw them out of a hat. These spiritual gifts are specific. He gives specific spiritual gifts to specific people. Why? Because God equips us with these specific spiritual gifts so we can join Him in the work of growing His Kingdom.

SCRIPTURE FOR TRUTH 8:
WE RECEIVE SPIRITUAL GIFTS

*Read these Scriptures and reflect upon
how We Receive Spiritual Gifts.*

If you, then, though you are evil, know how to give good gifts to your children, how much more will your Father in heaven give good gifts to those who ask him! — Matthew 7:11

Every good and perfect gift is from above, coming down from the Father of the heavenly lights, who does not change like shifting shadows. — James 1:17

There are different kinds of gifts, but the same Spirit distributes them. There are different kinds of service, but the same Lord. There are different kinds of working, but in all of them and in everyone it is the same God at work. Now to each one the manifestation of the Spirit is given for the common good. To one there is given through the Spirit a message of wisdom, to another a message of knowledge by means of the same Spirit, to another faith by the same Spirit, to another gifts of healing by that one Spirit, to another miraculous powers, to another prophecy, to another distinguishing between spirits, to another speaking in different kinds of tongues, and to still another the interpretation of tongues. All these are the work of one and the same Spirit, and he distributes them to each one, just as he determines. — 1 Corinthians 12:4-11

We have different gifts, according to the grace given to each of us. If your gift is prophesying, then prophesy in accordance with your faith; if it is serving, then serve; if it is teaching, then teach; if it is to encourage, then give encouragement; if it is giving, then give generously; if it is to lead, do it diligently; if it is to show mercy, do it cheerfully. — Romans 12:6-8

This salvation, which was first announced by the Lord, was confirmed to us by those who heard him. God also testified to it by signs, wonders and various miracles, and by gifts of the Holy Spirit distributed according to his will. — Hebrews 2:3-4

PRAY - READ - APPLY - MEMORIZE - SHARE

─────────── DAY 1 ───────────

Start your time by praising God for who He is—the Alpha and the Omega, the Beginning and the End, the Lord of lords, and the King of kings. Thank Him for loving you enough to send Jesus. Thank Jesus for loving you enough to die for your sin. Thank God for the gift of His Spirit. Thank Him for the specific spiritual gifts the Holy Spirit is cultivating within you. Pray that He will give you strength to develop the gifts He has entrusted to you.

If you haven't already read through the introductory comments for Truth 8, read them now. Underline, highlight, or make notes in the margin as you read.

Read through the Scriptures for Truth 8.

Close in prayer, asking God to open your eyes and quicken your heart to recognize the spiritual gifts He has given you.

─────────── DAY 2 ───────────

Start your time with God by acknowledging Him as the ultimate gift Giver.

Read aloud the verses for Truth 8 and reflect upon how We Receive Spiritual Gifts. Which verses resonate with you most? Identify a verse to memorize this week. Write it down here and begin memorizing it.

Answer these questions. Pray and think about how you can make application to your life.

- What are some of the favorite gifts you've received?

- What are some of the favorite gifts you've given?

- How do you think God feels about giving His children good gifts?

As you close your daily time with God in prayer, take time to make a list of the gifts you've experienced today. Let gratitude overflow into your day.

 **DAY 3**

Open your time with God today by opening your heart and mind to the deep truths He wants to reveal to you as you explore how We Receive Spiritual Gifts more completely.

Read again the verses for this week.

Rehearse your memory verse.

Answer these questions. Pray and think about how you can make application to your life.

- After reading the verses three times this week, which spiritual gifts do you feel God has given you? List them below. If you're not sure or you want to learn more, a simple Google search will point you to spiritual gifts assessments that can help you identify your spiritual gifts. A particularly good assessment (and it's free) can be found at https://gifts.churchgrowth.org/spiritual-gifts-survey/

- How are you developing those gifts?

As you close this time in prayer, imagine you are laying those spiritual gifts at your Father's throne. Offer the gifts you have received back to the Lord for His perfect use in places and in ways you cannot comprehend at this moment. Go forth with anticipation that God will surprise you with opportunities to bless others through the gifts He has already given you.

DAY 4

Begin with prayer, thanking God for what He is showing you already about this week's Truth, We Receive Spiritual Gifts.

Read the verses for the week again and underline every time the word *gift* or *gifts* is used. Circle every word that lists one of the spiritual gifts (faith, serving, etc.).

Practice your memory verse.

Answer these questions. Pray and think about how you can make application to your life.

- Before this week, how have you used one or more of your spiritual gifts?

- How have you used your gifts this week in a different situation or to bless someone new?

Choose one or two verses that have spoken deeply to you this week and pray them back to God as you close your time with Him.

—————— **DAY 5** ——————

Begin today's time with God by praying your memory verse back to Him.

Read again the verses for Truth 8.

Dig a little deeper into God's Word and find other passages that teach you about how We Receive Spiritual Gifts. List them here:

Close in prayer, thanking God for matching your spiritual gifts to you.

—————— DAY 6 ——————

Open your time with God with praise, repeating James 1:17 as a declaration of faith before the Lord.

Read the Scripture verses for Truth 8 again.

Review your memory verse.

List one or two times when you have truly sensed you were using your spiritual gifts to bless others. If you can identify a situation where a particular person was blessed by your gifts, list the person and the situation here.

1.

2.

Close with prayer, thanking God for preparing the way ahead of you every day so you may use the spiritual gifts He has given you.

—————— DAY 7 ——————

If you are meeting with a small group as part of this study, use this day for your group meeting.

Here is a possible outline for your time together as a group:

Open Your Hearts

- WORSHIP SONG: "I Surrender" — Hillsong Worship
- PRAYER: Encourage one or two people to offer a prayer of thanksgiving.
- SCRIPTURE: Ask one or two people to share the verse they memorized this week.

Discussion

1. What is one of the favorite gifts you have received? Why?

2. What is one of the favorite gifts you have given? Why?

3. Review I Corinthians 12:4-11 and Romans 12:6-8. What spiritual gifts have you been given? (If you took a spiritual gifts test this week as a part of Day 3, share what you learned.) How can you use these gifts to glorify God?

4. Where are some areas in your church that your spiritual gifts can be used?

5. Tell of a specific situation in which you were able to use one of your spiritual gifts. How did it bless others and how were you blessed?

6. Read I Corinthians 13:2. How are we to use our spiritual gifts?

Time of Commitment

- WORSHIP SONG: "I Give You My Heart" — Hillsong Worship
- PRAYER: Call upon one or two people to offer a prayer of commitment.

If you are not meeting with a small group, please take time on your own to go through the small group outline.

WE ARE EQUIPPED TO CONTINUE THE WORK OF JESUS AND GROW HIS KINGDOM

I find it interesting, to say the least, that the King of kings and the Lord of lords, the One who spoke and all creation came into being, would choose to use us to continue His work and grow His Kingdom.

His Kingdom is contrary to an earthly kingdom, which is represented by geography, by physical space on a map. For the people occupying that space on the map, the earthly king's word is law.

By contrast, God's Kingdom is in the heart of every human being who has willingly submitted themselves to the Lordship of Jesus Christ.

To grow His Kingdom is to make Him known, to point people to Jesus, to do His work, to help others choose Him as the only Lord and Savior of their lives! We do this individually as we live our lives for Him, and we do it corporately through the Church, which is the body of believers.

Obviously, we can't grow His Kingdom in our own power. So, we are equipped with spiritual gifts we are to nurture, develop, and use to make Him known. As humans, though, we frequently want what we don't have or what others have. We play this ugly game called *comparison*.

What I've learned about the comparison game is that most often, I lose.

Why? Because when we compare ourselves to others, we typically compare our "insides" to their "outsides." And, for most of us, our "insides" don't compare well to others' "outsides."

Why? Each of us is three people all at the same time. We have this *public* person within us. It's the person we project to everyone with whom we come in contact. It develops over time to protect who we really are and promote who we want to be in the eyes of others.

We also have this *private* person within us. It's the person we only let our family and close friends see. It's typically not as polite as the *public* person. It's more vulnerable. It's crankier. It's sillier. It's different in some very important ways from the *public* person.

Then, we have this *personal* person within us. It's the person whose thoughts and sometimes actions we would never want others to know. It's the person we, at times, are embarrassed to admit resides within us.

There is always a gap between our *personal* person and our *public* person. May I suggest that our character can be measured by the breadth of that gap? The greater the gap, the less the character. The narrower the gap, the greater the character. My favorite definition of character is "who you are when no one is looking."

So, how does this connect to spiritual gifts? Embrace the gifts God has given you, not the gifts you think you want or the gifts you admire in others. Quit comparing your gifts to the gifts of others. You are you! God created you exactly the way He intended. He equipped you with the specific gifts He needs you to have so that we can work individually, and collectively as the Church, to fulfill His purposes.

Get busy using *your* spiritual gifts.

SCRIPTURE FOR TRUTH 9:
WE ARE EQUIPPED TO CONTINUE
THE WORK OF JESUS
AND GROW HIS KINGDOM

Read these Scriptures and reflect upon how
We Are Equipped to Continue the Work
of Jesus and Grow His Kingdom.

So it is with you. Since you are eager for gifts of the Spirit, try to excel in those that build up the church. — 1 Corinthians 14:12

For we are God's handiwork, created in Christ Jesus to do good works, which God prepared in advance for us to do. — Ephesians 2:10

But you will receive power when the Holy Spirit comes on you; and you will be my witnesses in Jerusalem, and in all Judea and Samaria, and to the ends of the earth. — Acts 1:8

So Christ himself gave the apostles, the prophets, the evangelists, the pastors and teachers, to equip his people for works of service, so that the body of Christ may be built up until we all reach unity in the faith and in the knowledge of the Son of God and become mature, attaining to the whole measure of the fullness of Christ. — Ephesians 4:11-13

Therefore go and make disciples of all nations, baptizing them in the name of the Father and of the Son and of the Holy Spirit, and teaching them to obey everything I have commanded you. And surely I am with you always, to the very end of the age. — Matthew 28:19-20

PRAY - READ - APPLY - MEMORIZE - SHARE

―――――― DAY 1 ――――――

Praise God for who He is, the I Am who I Am, the Holy One, worthy of all praise and honor and glory. Thank Him for giving you the spiritual gifts He has given to you. Thank Him for wanting to use you to make a difference. Ask for forgiveness for playing the comparison game. Ask for courage to close the gap between who you are deep inside and who you are on the outside. Pray for an authentic and sincere heart that grows in love for Him and His creation.

If you haven't already read through the introductory comments for Truth 9, read them now. Underline, highlight, or make notes in the margin as you read.

Read through the Scriptures for Truth 9.

Close in prayer, thanking God for being a good, good Father and for equipping you with the gifts you need to be useful in growing His Kingdom.

―――――― DAY 2 ――――――

Start your time with God by praising Him for His creative ability and thanking Him for creating you exactly as you are with the specific spiritual gifts He has chosen for you.

Read aloud the Scriptures for Truth 9 and reflect upon how We Are Equipped to Continue the Work of Jesus and Grow His Kingdom. Which verses resonate with you most? Identify a verse to memorize this week. Write it down here and begin memorizing it.

Answer these questions. Pray and think about how you can make them apply to your life.

- Why do you think God chooses to use followers of Christ to help grow His Kingdom?

- How frequently do you play the comparison game?

- What things cause you to repeatedly compare yourself to other people?

As you close your daily time with God in prayer, thank Him for gifting you and using you just as you are. Ask Him to help you see yourself as He sees you: created and gifted just as He intended.

——————— DAY 3 ———————

Start with a prayer of praise and thanksgiving. Ask God to give you insights into your true character.

Read again the Scriptures for this week.

Rehearse your memory verse.

Answer these questions. Pray and think about how you can make them apply to your life.

- How would you describe your *public* person?

- How is your *private* person different from your *public* person?

- In what ways are you embarrassed by your *personal* person?

- How big is the gap between your *public* and *personal* person?

- What three things can you do to close the gap a little? What things should you do?

Close in prayer by asking God to continue revealing your true character and to give you courage, discipline, and commitment as you take specific steps to "close the gap."

DAY 4

Begin your time with God today in praise. Ask Him for clarity on how He wants you to use your spiritual gifts.

Read again the Scriptures for this week.

Practice your memory verse.

Answer these questions. Pray and think about how you can make them apply to your life.

- How is God calling you to use the spiritual gifts He has given you?

- How is God using you to make Him known and grow His Kingdom?

Close in prayer by thanking God for letting you join Him in His work. Pray for "divine appointments" with people whose hearts are ready to hear about the love of Jesus.

DAY 5

Begin with prayer, thanking God for what He is showing you already about this week's Truth, We Are Equipped to Continue the Work of Jesus and Grow His Kingdom. Pray your memory verse to Him.

Read again the verses for Truth 9.

Dig a little deeper into God's Word and find other passages that teach you about the Truth: We Are Equipped to Continue the Work of Jesus and Grow His Kingdom. List them here:

Pick your favorite verse from this week's Scriptures and pray it back to God today.

—————————— **DAY 6** ——————————

Open your prayer time by praising God for equipping other followers of Christ with gifts and abilities as you serve alongside them in His Kingdom work.

Read the Scriptures for Truth 9 again.

Review your memory verse.

Think of ways you are making God known to other people. List a few of those situations below.

Close with prayer.

—————————— **DAY 7** ——————————

If you are meeting with a small group as part of this study, use this day for your group meeting.

Here is a possible outline for your time together as a group:

Open Your Hearts

- WORSHIP SONG: "What a Beautiful Name" — Hillsong Worship

- PRAYER: Have one or two people to offer a prayer of thanksgiving.

- SCRIPTURE: Encourage one or two people to share the verse they memorized this week.

Discussion:

1. Why do you think God chooses to use followers of Christ to help grow His Kingdom?

2. Discuss some of the things that cause us to compare ourselves to others.

3. How does comparison affect our everyday lives?

4. Read the paragraphs about your *private, personal,* and *public* person in the commentary for Truth 9. What are some ways you can close the gap a little between your *private* and *personal* person? What about between your *personal* and *public* person?

5. What are some other Scriptures you found this week that teach the Truth, We Are Equipped to Continue the Work of Jesus and Grow His Kingdom?

6. Share some ways you are making God known to other people.

Time of Commitment

- WORSHIP SONG: "You Say" — Lauren Daigle
- PRAYER: Take a moment for each person to silently pray through the following:
  - » Thank God for using you to further His Kingdom.
  - » Thank Him for the spiritual gifts, abilities, and talents He has given you.
  - » Thank Him for the situations and places in which He has placed you to use these gifts, abilities, and talents.

- » Ask for forgiveness for comparing yourself to others.

- » Thank God for the gifts, abilities, and talents of others in the group.

- » Ask for courage to close the gap between who you are on the inside and who you are on the outside.

- » Pray that God will reveal to you how you are to use all He has made you to be to help grow His Kingdom.

- » Pray Ephesians 2:10, thanking God that you are His handiwork, created in Christ Jesus to do the good works He has already prepared for you!

- Have one person to close the prayer time by offering a prayer of commitment.

If you are not meeting with a small group, please take time on your own to go through the small group outline.

WE EXERCISE
OUR GIFTS IN
OBEDIENCE AND LOVE

Obedience. Why is it that for many of us a wall of resistance starts to form when we think of obeying anyone?

I think part of it is the deep-seated independence residing in each of us. We all need a certain amount of independence. At the same time, we hopefully develop a healthy enough ego that allows us to submit ourselves to others at the appropriate times.

Years ago, I taught a college Bible study at my church. I rotated teaching with Dr. Todd Still, who is now the dean of Truett Seminary in Waco, Texas. At the time, however, Todd was teaching at Dallas Baptist University. He and his wife, Carolyn, were members of our church in Arlington, Texas. One morning, Todd said to the group something along the lines of: God's will for your life is the same as it is for mine, and yours, and yours, and yours [as he pointed to multiple people in the audience]. His will is that we be obedient. He may call you to one thing and me to another, but His will is that we be obedient.

Todd's words got my attention. Knowing God's will for my life had been important to me for a long time. In my younger years, I had this idea that His will was something I was supposed to discern, and it would be a certain career I was to pursue for a lifetime. Todd's statement prompted me to start processing the concept of God's will for my life in a fresh way. As I obey God, I live in His will on a daily basis. It took the pressure off; I no longer felt driven to make one big decision that was supposed to last a lifetime.

So, if His will is that we be obedient, with what are we being obedient and how are we living out that obedience specifically? I've come to believe we are to be obedient day by day, moment by moment, using the gifts God has given us for His glory. God gives them to us for His purposes, not for our pride and egos.

We are also to use the gifts in love. The Gospel writer, Mark, tells us a story about a teacher of the law who asks Jesus, "Of all the commandments, which is the most important?" (Mark 12:28). Do you remember Jesus' answer?

> *"The most important one," answered Jesus, "is this: 'Hear, O Israel: The Lord our God, the Lord is one. Love the Lord your God with all your heart and with all your soul and with all your mind and with all your strength.' The second is this: 'Love your neighbor as yourself.' There is no commandment greater than these."* (Mark 12:29-31).

One morning, I read this passage in my chronological Bible and began to pray that God would teach me to love Him with all my heart, soul, mind, and strength and to love others as I love myself.

Not long after that, I read about the night before Jesus was crucified in John 13:34. Jesus was eating around a table with His disciples. Very loosely translated, Jesus said to His disciples, "Boys, listen up. I've got a new command for you. From now on, I want you to love others as I have loved you these last three years. You've been with me, experienced my love, so now go love others as I have loved you."

It occurred to me upon reading John 13:34 that loving the way Jesus loves is a whole lot different than loving as I love myself. (Just call me Captain Obvious.) For followers of Christ, this is really the expectation. Everyone can and should love others as they love themselves. You don't have to be a Christian to understand that concept. However, without Jesus, without the Holy Spirit taking up residence within us, there is no way we love as He loves. Even as mature Christians, we find this very difficult if not impossible. Yet, it's exactly what Jesus told the apostles that night.

In fact, imagine our world, our churches, our families if we as Christians really learned to love as Jesus loves! Before we can do that, though, we have to know how Jesus loves. His disciples knew. They had lived with Him every day for three years. But do we really know how Jesus loves?

Paul gave us the best insight into how Jesus loves when he wrote 1 Corinthians 13. You will read it in the Scriptures for this Truth. As you read, please take it very slowly. Stop on each descriptive word in that passage and ask yourself, "Do I love this way? Am I patient… kind? Do I encourage others or envy them? Do I boast? Am I proud? Do I lift people up or dishonor them? Am I selfish or selfless? Am I easily angered? Do I forgive, or do I keep a record of wrongs? Do I delight in evil or rejoice in the truth? Do I protect? Do I trust? Do I hope? Do I persevere?"

During a community worship service, I heard Pastor Jason Paredes, lead pastor at Fielder Church in Arlington, Texas, say, "*Loving as Jesus loves means we give people what they need the most, when they least deserve it, at great personal cost to ourselves.*" Wow! What a great way to sum up loving as Jesus loves.

As Christians, can we do a better job loving those around us? Yes, of course! And it includes those who don't know Jesus, those with whom we are acquaintances, as well as friends we haven't met yet. It also includes those closest to us—our families, our dearest friends, those with whom we go to church. Again, imagine our churches today, our families, our communities, our country, and the world if we, as Christians, prayed every day for the Holy Spirit to teach us to love as He loves and genuinely worked to live it out in every single relationship!

Be careful, though, when you earnestly seek to love as He loves. In my experience, you will get the opportunity to love some people who are hard to love. It's good for us, though. It actually helps us to see ways in which we make it hard for others to love us. It promotes growth and maturity within us, and it blesses others.

Exercising our spiritual gifts and talents is a critical part of our journey. After all, these gifts and talents have been given to us to grow and build His Kingdom. We have a responsibility to use and develop our spiritual gifts for His purposes. At the same time, God is just as concerned about the manner in which we use them. Are we obedient? Do we exercise them in love, for the benefit of others, or with a sense of pride that hopes to bring attention to ourselves? Are we using our gifts for service to Him and to His creation, or has the use of our gifts moved from service to performance?[12]

SCRIPTURE FOR TRUTH 10: WE EXERCISE OUR GIFTS IN OBEDIENCE AND LOVE

*Read these Scriptures and reflect upon how
We Exercise Our Gifts in Obedience and Love.*

Does the LORD delight in burnt offerings and sacrifices as much as in obeying the LORD? To obey is better than sacrifice, and to heed is better than the fat of rams.— 1 Samuel 15:22

Walk in obedience to all that the LORD your God has commanded you, so that you may live and prosper and prolong your days in the land that you will possess. — Deuteronomy 5:33

And now, Israel, what does the LORD your God ask of you but to fear the LORD your God, to walk in obedience to him, to love him, to serve the LORD your God with all your heart and with all your soul — Deuteronomy 10:12

And what does the LORD require of you? To act justly and to love mercy and to walk humbly with your God. — Micah 6:8

A new command I give you: Love one another. As I have loved you, so you must love one another. By this everyone will know that you are my disciples, if you love one another. — John 13:34-35

If I speak in the tongues of men or of angels, but do not have love, I am only a resounding gong or a clanging cymbal. If I have the gift of prophecy and can fathom all mysteries and all knowledge, and if I have a faith that can move mountains, but do not have love, I am nothing. If I give all I possess to the poor and give over my body to hardship that I may boast, but do not have love, I gain nothing. Love is patient, love is kind. It does not envy, it does not boast, it is not proud. It does not dishonor others, it is not self-seeking, it is not easily angered, it keeps no record of wrongs. Love does not delight in evil but rejoices with the truth. It always protects, always trusts, always hopes, always perseveres. Love never fails. But where there are prophecies, they will cease; where there are tongues, they will be stilled; where there is knowledge, it will pass

away. For we know in part and we prophesy in part, but when complete-
ness comes, what is in part disappears. When I was a child, I talked like
a child, I thought like a child, I reasoned like a child. When I became
a man, I put the ways of childhood behind me. For now we see only
a reflection as in a mirror; then we shall see face to face. Now I know
in part; then I shall know fully, even as I am fully known. And now
these three remain: faith, hope and love. But the greatest of these is love.
— 1 Corinthians 13:1-13

PRAY – READ – APPLY – MEMORIZE – SHARE

──────────── DAY 1 ────────────

Begin by praising God for who He is, the all-knowing, all-encompassing, ever-present Lord in your life. Thank God for life with Him every day. Ask for His courage to help you obey, to do what's right, regardless. Ask Jesus to teach you how to love Him with all your heart, soul, mind, and strength. Ask Him to teach you to love others the way He loves them. Ask for forgiveness for pride and ego that get in the way of your obedience and love.

If you haven't already read through the introductory comments of Truth 10, read them now. Underline, highlight, or make notes in the margin as you read.

Read through the Scriptures for Truth 10.

As you close in prayer, commit to loving the Lord with a renewed passion and with all your heart, soul, mind, and strength today.

──────────── DAY 2 ────────────

Open your time with God by thanking Him for His consistent love for you.

Read aloud the Truth 10 Scriptures and reflect upon how We Exercise Our Gifts in Obedience and Love. Which verses resonate with you most? Identify a verse to memorize this week. Write it down here and begin memorizing it.

Answer these questions. Pray and think about how you can make application to your life.

- On a scale of 1-10, 10 being 100%, how would you rate your obedience to God right now?

- In what parts of your life are you not being obedient?

As you close your daily time with God in prayer, spend some time before the Lord and take the first step in obedience by submitting every part of your life to Him.

DAY 3

Open your prayer time with praise.

Read again the Scriptures for this week.

Rehearse your memory verse.

Answer these questions. Pray and think about how you can make application to your life.

- In what ways is it hard for you to obey God in the everyday matters of life?

- What are some steps you can take to submit every part of your life to Him and earnestly seek to be completely obedient?

As you close in prayer, ask God to give you the courage and discipline to choose commitment to the steps you just wrote down which will help you be more obedient.

──────── DAY 4 ────────

As you begin your time with God today, follow the words of Psalm 9:2: "*I will be glad and rejoice in you; I will sing the praises of your name, O Most High.*"

Read again the Scriptures for this week.

Practice your memory verse.

Answer these questions. Pray and think about how you can make application to your life.

- When you read the descriptive words in 1 Corinthians 13 about how Jesus loves, which three are the easiest for you? Why?

- When you read about how Jesus loves in 1 Corinthians 13, which three are the most difficult for you? Why?

- What can you do to improve your ability to love as He loves in those three ways?

Make this a practical exercise this week, and ask God to reveal to you the name of one person you have a hard time loving. Commit to pursuing obedience to God as you seek to love this person.

Close in prayer, rejoicing again and singing His praises. Ask the Lord to give you strength to love the person you just identified as He loves them.

DAY 5

Begin today's time with God by praying your memory verse back to Him.

Read again the verses for Truth 10.

Dig a little deeper into God's Word and find other passages that teach you about the Truth: We Exercise Our Gifts in Love and Obedience. List them here:

Pick your favorite verse from this week's Scriptures and pray it back to God today as you close in prayer.

DAY 6

Look to the Psalms and find several verses of praise to read back to the Father as you open your time in His presence.

Read the Scriptures for Truth 10 again.

Review your memory verse.

What fresh insights have you seen in these Scriptures as you have read them every day this week?

Close with prayer.

DAY 7

If you are meeting with a small group as part of this study, use this day for your group meeting.

Here is a possible outline for your time together as a group:

Open Your Hearts

- WORSHIP SONG: "Love God Love People" — Danny Gokey

- PRAYER: Offer prayers of thanksgiving.

- SCRIPTURE: Request that one or two people share the memory verse they learned this week.

Discussion

1. In what areas of your life is it most challenging to be obedient?

2. What are some steps you can take to submit these areas to God and earnestly seek to be obedient?

3. Read aloud I Corinthians 13:1-13. Identify and emphasize each word describing the way Jesus loves.

4. Share descriptive words from 1 Corinthians 13 that are easy for you. Why?

5. Share words that are the most difficult. Why?

6. What can you do to improve your ability to love as Jesus loves in those which are the most difficult for you?

7. What fresh insights have you seen in the Scriptures for Truth 10 as you have read them each day?

Time of Commitment

- WORSHIP SONG: "Trust and Obey" — Big Daddy Weave
- PRAYER: Divide into groups of 3-4 to pray for one another in these areas:
  - » Places in your life you struggle with obedience
  - » Courage and strength to be obedient
  - » Someone you have a particularly difficult time loving
  - » Areas in your life you have trouble loving as Jesus loves
  - » Commitment to improve the way you love

If you are not meeting with a small group, please take time on your own to go through the small group outline.

WE GROW IN THE LORD EXPERIENCING SPIRITUAL FORMATION AND MATURITY

As we pursue a healthy relationship with Jesus and exercise our spiritual gifts in obedience and love, we are formed spiritually. We mature in our faith. We grow, and we become more and more spiritually mature. In Christian terminology, it is the process of *sanctification*— becoming more like Christ—becoming holy in His sight.

Mother Teresa said, "Holiness does not consist in doing extraordinary things. It consists in accepting, with a smile, what Jesus sends us. It consists in accepting and following the will of God."[13]

Accepting Him, choosing Jesus, is just the first step. However, we cannot stop there. We are to grow and mature in our relationship with Jesus, which helps us to become more like Him so that He can use us for His purposes.

We can equate it to being an infant. We have life at the point of conception. We mature within our mothers' wombs until we are born. As infants, we are 100 percent selfish. All our thoughts and actions are focused on ourselves. We have no consideration for anyone else in the world! Ideally and hopefully, as we grow and mature, we become less selfish. We become more "others-focused."

In a similar way, as we mature in Christ, as we are formed spiritually, we are less and less concerned about ourselves and our selfish desires. We become more and more concerned with the desires of Christ. We sacrifice our desires for His. We can care more for others because we are thoroughly cared for by Him. We choose commitment to Him in the everyday.

Every day, many times a day, we encounter a proverbial "fork in the road" in various areas of our lives. You know that fork, right? It's the fork where you know what you *should* do, but it's not what you *want* to do. That fork! It's at that fork where you have the opportunity to choose commitment or choose compromise.

To be clear, I don't mean the compromise that says, "I'll meet you halfway." Nor do I mean the type of compromise reached by two people or two sides, who, after thoughtful and meaningful conversation, come to an agreement on a topic of significance. I mean the negative side of compromise that robs us of our commitments or convictions and takes us down a path we know to be destructive to ourselves and to those around us.

Imagine our world today if we consistently chose commitment over compromise.

- What if husbands and wives chose commitment over compromise?

- What if moms and dads chose commitment over compromise?

- What if family members chose commitment over compromise?

- What if friends chose commitment over compromise?

- What if employers chose commitment over compromise?

- What if employees chose commitment over compromise?

- What if mature, spiritually formed Christians chose commitment over compromise … in all areas of life?

If we consistently chose commitment over compromise, what would happen?

- Would our families be stronger?

- How about our churches?

- How about our communities?

- Would there be more authenticity?

- Would there be more unity?

- Would there be more trust?

- Would the gospel be spreading at a faster rate?

- Would more people come to life with Jesus because more Christians would be living and loving as Jesus lived and loved?

- Would we be less hypocritical and more genuine, revealing more of the vulnerability that resides in each of us?

- Would our lives point more people to Jesus?

As we mature through spiritual formation, we gain more courage and discipline to do what's right, regardless of the cost or consequences, regardless of the sacrifice or suffering, regardless of the fear or the fright. Regardless of anything at all, we consistently choose commitment over compromise.

We recognize that God's desires are more important than our own, which means we are more likely to release our selfish desires and focus on what is best for others. We have a better perspective on the important compared to the trivial.

Why is it that we, even as believers, teachers, deacons, elders, priests, or pastors, can take the trivial and make it important? Because we are human. Because we have a sinful nature. Because we are easily distracted from focusing on Him to focusing on ourselves.

When we take the trivial and raise it to a level of importance higher than it deserves, we create an idol and commit idolatry. David, in Psalm 16:4, reminds us that our sorrows are multiplied when we pursue other gods over the one true God. How many of us are caught in this pattern? Maybe all of us. Even as mature believers, we can get sidetracked and raise the trivial to important.

Scripture teaches that we are to pursue maturity in our faith and in our spiritual gifts so we may build up the body of Christ in unity and in love (Ephesians 4:14-16). This pursuit of spiritual formation and maturity, which comes from His love for us and our love for Him, produces wisdom—wisdom of the heart and wisdom in the moment.

Wisdom of the heart is born out of the *"fear of the LORD."* Solomon writes in Proverbs 1:7: *"The fear of the LORD is the beginning of knowledge, but fools despise wisdom and instruction."*

Solomon was the son of King David and Bathsheba. He was anointed as king of Israel shortly before the death of his father. Upon becoming king, God told Solomon he could ask for anything he wanted, and God would grant it.

Seriously? Wow! What would you ask for? Money. Fame. Power. Good health.

Let's see what Solomon asked for: *"So give your servant a discerning heart to govern your people and to distinguish between right and wrong"* (1 Kings 3:9).

How did God respond? *"The Lord was pleased that Solomon had asked for this. So God said to him, 'Since you have asked for this and not for long life or wealth for yourself, nor have asked for the death of your enemies but for discernment in administering justice, I will do what you have asked. I will give you a wise and discerning heart"* (1 Kings 3:10-12).

Years later, Solomon wrote the lion's share of the book of Proverbs. Again, in Proverbs 9:10, Solomon tells us the beginning of wisdom is the *"fear of the LORD."* What is the fear of the Lord? Simply stated, it is a healthy awe, reverence, and respect for the Lord that produces a desire to obey Him.

The commentary in my NIV *Life Application Study Bible* says it this way: "In this age of information, knowledge is plentiful, but wisdom is scarce. Wisdom means far more than simply knowing a lot. It is a basic attitude that affects every aspect of life. The foundation of knowledge is to fear the Lord—to honor and respect God, to live in awe of his power, and to obey his Word. Faith in God should be the controlling principle for your understanding of the world, your attitudes, and your actions. Trust in God—he will make you truly wise."[14]

This is *wisdom of the heart* and it produces *wisdom in the moment*, which is the wisdom, the discernment, to know what to do or not do, what to say or not say, in any given situation.

You see, true wisdom is about the heart more than it is about the mind. It is the God-given wisdom to see as He sees, hear as He hears, encourage as He encourages, and love as He loves.

SCRIPTURE FOR TRUTH 11: WE GROW IN THE LORD EXPERIENCING SPIRITUAL FORMATION AND MATURITY

Read these Scriptures and reflect upon how We Grow in the Lord Experiencing Spiritual Formation and Maturity.

I planted the seed, Apollos watered it, but God has been making it grow. So neither the one who plants nor the one who waters is anything, but only God, who makes things grow. — 1 Corinthians 3:6-7

Then we will no longer be infants, tossed back and forth by the waves, and blown here and there by every wind of teaching and by the cunning and craftiness of people in their deceitful scheming. Instead, speaking the truth in love, we will grow to become in every respect the mature body of him who is the head, that is, Christ. From him the whole body, joined and held together by every supporting ligament, grows and builds itself up in love, as each part does its work. — Ephesians 4:14-16

We ought always to thank God for you, brothers and sisters, and rightly so, because your faith is growing more and more, and the love all of you have for one another is increasing. — 2 Thessalonians 1:3

Therefore, rid yourselves of all malice and all deceit, hypocrisy, envy, and slander of every kind. Like newborn babies, crave pure spiritual milk, so that by it you may grow up in your salvation, now that you have tasted that the Lord is good. — 1 Peter 2:1-3

But grow in the grace and knowledge of our Lord and Savior Jesus Christ. — 2 Peter 3:18

PRAY – READ – APPLY – MEMORIZE – SHARE

———————— DAY 1 ————————

Begin by praising God for who He is. He is the good, good Father, the Giver of all good and perfect things. Thank Him for loving you enough to expect more from you, for loving you enough to not allow you to stay as you are but to lead you to growth so He can use your life and your abilities for His good purposes. Ask Him to give you courage to choose commitment over compromise as you encounter the "forks in the road" that will surely come today.

If you haven't already read through the introductory comments for Truth 11, read them now. Underline, highlight, or make notes in the margin as you read.

Read through the Scriptures for Truth 11.

Close in prayer, thanking God for His patience to lead you toward spiritual maturity.

———————— DAY 2 ————————

Open your time with God by praising His name and offering your adoration.

Read aloud the verses for Truth 11 and reflect upon how We Grow in the Lord Experiencing Spiritual Formation and Maturity. Which verses resonate with you most? Identify a verse to memorize this week. Write it down here and begin memorizing it.

Answer these questions. Pray and think about how you can apply them to your life.

- On a scale of 1-10, how would you rate your spiritual maturity?

- In what ways are you prone to make the trivial important?

To close your time with God today, commit to letting God have full control of your life so His priorities become your priorities.

DAY 3

Open your prayer time with praise.

Read the verses again for this week.

Rehearse your memory verse.

Answer these questions. Pray and think about how you can apply them to your life.

- At what "forks in the road" of your life, do you continually choose compromise over commitment? Why?

- At what "forks in the road" of your life, do you continually choose commitment over compromise? Why?

- What are some things you can do to help you choose commitment over compromise more consistently?

Close in prayer, making a commitment to recognize compromise in its many forms today—and to choose commitment instead. Pray for His strength to choose well.

DAY 4

Thank God for His never-ending love as you open your time with Him.

Read the verses again for this week.

Practice your memory verse.

Answer these questions. Pray and think about how you can apply them to your life.

- In what ways do you contribute to the unity and love within your:

  » Family

  » Friends

  » Coworkers

  » Church

- In what ways do you distract from the unity and love within your:

» Family

» Friends

» Coworkers

» Church

Close in prayer, praying for unity and love in the relationships you considered today.

 **DAY 5**

Open with prayer, seeking to *"grow in the grace and knowledge of our Lord and Savior Jesus Christ"* (2 Peter 3:18) as you meet with God today. Pray your memory verse to the Father.

Read the verses again for Truth 11.

Dig a little deeper into God's Word and find other passages that teach you about the Truth: We Grow in the Lord Experiencing Spiritual Formation and Maturity. List them here:

Pick your favorite verse from this week's Scriptures and pray it back to God today as you close in prayer.

———————— **DAY 6** ————————

Open your time with God in praise.

Read the verses for Truth 11 again.

Review your memory verse.

What three steps will you take to proactively mature in your faith?

Close with prayer, committing to the Lord those three steps you will take to grow your faith toward maturity.

———————— **DAY 7** ————————

If you are meeting with a small group as part of this study, use this day for your group meeting.

Here is a possible outline for your time together as a group:

Open Your Hearts

- WORSHIP SONG: "Psalm 42" — Tori Kelly
- PRAYER: Ask one or two people to offer a prayer of thanksgiving.
- SCRIPTURE: Encourage one or two people to share the verse they memorized this week.

Discussion

1. In what ways are you prone to make the trivial important? Why?

2. Share a time you were faced with a "fork in the road," and even though it was difficult, chose commitment over compromise. What helped you to make this choice?

3. At what "forks in the road" do you struggle to choose commitment over compromise? Why?

4. Discuss some things you can do to choose commitment over compromise.

5. Read Ephesians 4:14-16. In what ways do you contribute to the unity and love within your:

   • Family

   • Friends

   • Coworkers

   • Church

   • Other

6. In what ways do you distract from unity and love in these areas?

7. Discuss some ways to proactively grow your faith toward maturity.

Time of Commitment

- WORSHIP SONG: "The Blessing" — Kari Jobe/Cody Carnes, Elevation Worship

- PRAYER: Have an open prayer time for multiple people to pray for courage, commitment, unity, and love.

If you are not meeting with a small group, please take time on your own to go through the small group outline.

Our Gifts Develop and We Bear Fruit

As the Holy Spirit takes up residence in our hearts, He begins to polish out the cracks in them that were created by sin. Think about your heart as a mirror. Think about sin as cracking that mirror. As Christians, we are called and equipped to continue the work of Jesus and to grow His Kingdom. That means we are to point people to Christ and to help those who already know Him to grow in their faith and their obedience. However, if our lives, our speech, our attitudes, and our behavior consistently point in a different direction, we have no credibility with which to point people to Jesus. In fact, when people perceive our behavior as being inconsistent with our claim to be followers of Christ, we actually push people away from Christ!

If we are going to reach the world for Christ, we must start with our own hearts. We begin by accepting Jesus as Savior. We continue daily in earnest prayer to ask the Holy Spirit to permeate our hearts. As He does, the Spirit polishes out the cracks. What happens to your reflection in the mirror when the mirror is filled with cracks? It's distorted, and it's the same with our hearts. When our hearts are full of sinful cracks, we reflect a distorted image of Christ and push people away from Him. However, as the Holy Spirit polishes out the cracks, we reflect a truer and purer image of who Jesus really is. Then the people we encounter, the people with whom we live life, are drawn to Him. We bear fruit.

As the Holy Spirit occupies more and more space in our hearts, the desire to obey and please Him grows. We spend more time with Him and in His Word.

What pleases Him pleases us. What hurts Him hurts us. What burdens the heart of God starts to burden our hearts. As He burdens our hearts, we begin to see the God-given vision He has for our lives. To paraphrase Dr. John C. Maxwell as he writes in *The Maxwell Leadership Bible*: a God-given vision is born out of a burden God places on our hearts.[15]

This vision for how God wants to use our lives motivates us to use the spiritual gifts He's given us. We start to recognize the gifts we have and why we have those gifts. As we use them and learn more about them, they develop... they mature. Others start to recognize these gifts in us. Some are drawn to Christ as we use our gifts. Those who already know Christ are blessed by the way we use our gifts and actually grow in the Lord by being blessed through our gifts. We bear fruit.

When I think about bearing fruit, the first person who comes to my mind is my dad. Except for the four years I was at Baylor University, my dad was my pastor from 1962 to 1999. In 1999, he resigned as pastor of First Baptist Church of Arlington to serve as the executive director for Texas Baptists. It was a new day for him. He had been pastoring churches for decades because he began pastoring at the age of fifteen! My grandad, J. W. Wade, was a pastor in Woodward, Oklahoma, at that time. Many country churches all over northwest Oklahoma needed preachers in 1955, so my grandmother would drive her fifteen-year-old son (my dad) to these churches on Sunday mornings so he could preach for them.

As you can imagine, my dad's spiritual gifts of preaching, teaching, leading, and serving were fairly immature at age fifteen. However, he faithfully and obediently began to exercise those gifts. He studied, he worked, he learned, and he developed the gifts God gave him. It was a journey that continues even to this day. At seventy-nine years of age, he still uses his gifts. He preaches, he teaches, he leads, he serves. Countless lives have been changed for the better. People are in Heaven right now because of the work of the Holy Spirit and the spiritual gifts that my dad uses so faithfully. People are stronger, more mature Christians because my dad has faithfully and obediently lived out his calling using the spiritual gifts the Holy Spirit has entrusted to him. He continues to bear fruit.

A healthy vine leads to a healthy branch, which leads to healthy fruit that blesses people. May we be found faithful and therefore fruitful!

SCRIPTURE FOR TRUTH 12: OUR GIFTS DEVELOP AND WE BEAR FRUIT

Read these Scriptures and reflect upon how
Our Gifts Develop and We Bear Fruit.

I am the true vine, and my Father is the gardener. He cuts off every branch in me that bears no fruit, while every branch that does bear fruit he prunes so that it will be even more fruitful. You are already clean because of the word I have spoken to you. Remain in me, as I also remain in you. No branch can bear fruit by itself; it must remain in the vine. Neither can you bear fruit unless you remain in me. I am the vine; you are the branches. If you remain in me and I in you, you will bear much fruit; apart from me you can do nothing. If you do not remain in me, you are like a branch that is thrown away and withers; such branches are picked up, thrown into the fire and burned. If you remain in me and my words remain in you, ask whatever you wish, and it will be done for you. This is to my Father's glory, that you bear much fruit, showing yourselves to be my disciples. — John 15:1-8

You did not choose me, but I chose you and appointed you so that you might go and bear fruit—fruit that will last — John 15:16

So that you may live a life worthy of the Lord and please him in every way: bearing fruit in every good work, growing in the knowledge of God — Colossians 1:10

PRAY – READ – APPLY – MEMORIZE – SHARE

DAY 1

Offer a word of praise to the Father, the Son, and the Holy Spirit for He is the Giver of all good and perfect things. He spoke and all things came into being. He breathed the breath of life into you. He is faithful and true. Thank Him for His loving patience in your life as He has been polishing out the cracks left behind by sin.

If you haven't already read through the introductory comments for Truth 12, read them now. Underline, highlight, or make notes in the margin as you read.

Read through the Scriptures for Truth 12.

As you close in prayer, commit before God to reflect a truer and purer image of who Jesus really is.

DAY 2

Open with prayer, thanking God for allowing you to join Him in growing His Kingdom.

Read aloud the Scriptures for Truth 12 and reflect upon how Our Gifts Develop and We Bear Fruit. Which verses resonate with you most? Identify a verse to memorize this week. Write it down here and begin memorizing it.

Answer these questions. Pray and think about how you will be able to apply them in your life.

- What burdens your heart?

- What has God revealed to you about that burden?

Close your time with the Lord by asking for His help in developing the gifts He has given you.

——————— DAY 3 ———————

Begin your time with God by thanking Him for gifting you so that you may participate in His Kingdom plan. Ask for providential appointments that will give you the opportunity to influence well and bear healthy fruit for His glory. Ask for protection against your own selfish pride and ego that try to rob God of the glory due to Him.

Read the Scriptures again for this week.

Rehearse your memory verse.

Answer these questions. Pray and think about how you will be able to apply them in your life.

- What are your spiritual gifts?

- How are you developing them?

Close in prayer by specifically thanking God for the gifts He has given to you. Imagine you are placing each of those gifts before His throne as a commitment to use them for holy purposes. Ask for His wisdom and insight to understand how to use your gifts today.

Today, open your time with the Lord by opening God's Word. Turn to Psalms and find three verses of praise to echo back to your Heavenly Father.

Read the Scriptures again for this week.

Practice your memory verse.

Answer these questions. Pray and think about how you will be able to apply them in your life.

- How are you using your spiritual gifts?

- What kind of fruit are you seeing?

Before you close in prayer, think back over the past twenty-four hours since you prayed yesterday's closing prayer. You placed your spiritual gifts before His throne as a commitment to use them for God's Kingdom purposes. Reflect on the ways you were able to use your gifts to bless others in the span of one day. Now, close in prayer, thanking God for those divine appointments, and renew your commitment before His throne to use your gifts for God's good purposes.

--------- **DAY 5** ---------

Open with a prayer of praise and offer your memory verse to the Lord as a part of your prayer.

Read again the verses for Truth 12.

Dig a little deeper into God's Word and find other passages that teach you about the Truth: Our Gifts Develop and We Bear Fruit. List them here.

Pick your favorite verse from this week's Scriptures and pray it back to God today as you close in prayer.

--------- **DAY 6** ---------

Read Psalm 18:1-2 to God as you open your time in His Word today.

Read the Scriptures for Truth 12 again.

Review your memory verse.

Look at the John 15:1-8 passage more closely. There are three "If" statements spoken by Jesus. The first one has been filled into the following chart. Write out the other two "If" statements, separating the sentence segments into columns. (*Then* is implied in each of the sentences.)

IF	(THEN)
If you remain in Me and I in you,	you will bear much fruit; apart from Me you can do nothing.

Now that you have "dissected" these verses, what insights can you pull out of them?

In the last sentence of this passage, what does Jesus say brings glory to the Father?

That you _____ _____ _____.

Close in prayer, thanking God that He willingly and lovingly equips you with spiritual gifts so you may bear fruit to bring Him glory.

——————— DAY 7 ———————

If you are meeting with a small group as part of this study, use this day for your group meeting.

Here is a possible outline for your time together as a group:

Open Your Hearts

- WORSHIP SONG: "Oceans" — Hillsong UNITED
- PRAYER: Encourage one or two people to offer a prayer of praise.
- SCRIPTURE: Ask one or two people to share their memory verse for this week.

Discussion

1. Read aloud the Scriptures for Truth 12.

2. In Truth 9, we discussed spiritual gifts. Talk about your spiritual gifts and the steps you are taking to develop them.

3. What burdens your heart?

4. In what ways can you use your spiritual gifts to minister to people or in situations that burden your heart?

5. In what ways are you using your spiritual gifts now? What kind of fruit are you seeing?

6. Look at John 15:1-8 and discuss the if/then statements referenced in the chart for Day 6. What does Jesus tell us brings glory to the Father?

Time of Commitment

- WORSHIP SONG: "Way Maker" — Leeland

- PRAYER: Close with several people praying for:

  » Providential appointments that will give opportunities to influence well and bear healthy fruit

  » Protection against selfish pride, fear, or anything else that robs God of the glory due Him

  » Specific opportunities in which God can use us to grow His Kingdom

If you are not meeting with a small group, please take time on your own to go through the small group outline.

OUR LIVES ARE CHARACTERIZED BY THE FRUIT OF THE SPIRIT

Legacy. What kind of legacy do you want to leave? A few years ago, Pam and I began talking about legacy. In our minds, legacy relates to priorities. We want to leave a strong legacy in the areas of life that are priorities to us.

What are your priorities? Priorities, in some ways, change based on the season of life in which you currently live. As a newly married couple, one of our goals was to buy a house, so saving money became a priority. Through the years, we have set many goals and adjusted our priorities to meet those goals.

Ultimately, though, when I ask about your priorities, I'm asking about those things in your life over which nothing takes precedence. You know, there are some things in life that are so important about which we must refuse to fail. What are those things for you?

Faith, family, fitness, and finances encompass the priorities that Pam and I have set for ourselves. We have determined that, with the Lord's help, we will leave a strong legacy of faith, family, fitness, and finances. So, our daily lives are structured accordingly. Our goals align with our priorities. We pray for the Lord's courage to choose commitment every day so that we stay true to these priorities.

In the area of fitness, for example, we've decided that one of the best gifts we can give Caleb and Taylor is our health. When we don't feel like working out or eating correctly, we make an effort to shift our thoughts to why we are working out, why we are on a particular eating routine, and that helps us choose commitment in the moment...at that proverbial "fork in the road."

In his captivating book, *The 12 Week Year*, Brian Moran identifies that moment at which we choose commitment over compromise as being "great in the moment."[16] What happens when we are consistently great in the moment?

Within our priority of faith, it means we choose Jesus. It means we choose obedience. It means we choose commitment. It means we ask the Holy Spirit to permeate our hearts, our minds, our mouths. As we travel this daily journey of being great in the moment, our perspectives start to change. We begin to live life from a biblical perspective. We filter every decision through the question, "What does Scripture say?", which is similar to the popular "What would Jesus do?" Filtering every decision through Jesus and Scripture, as interpreted to us by the Holy Spirit, we live life from a biblical perspective.

Living every day with a biblical perspective informs our purpose, which informs our priorities, which informs our passions, which gives us perseverance and persistence, which produces fruit.[17] As we live life this way, the fruit of the Spirit starts to present itself in our daily lives. There is more love, joy, peace, and goodness in our lives. We tend to be more patient, kind, faithful, and gentle with ourselves and those around us. We exercise more self-control. Bottom line, we are blessed, and the fruit of the Spirit is on display in our lives.

Other than my time at Baylor, I've only had two pastors in my life: my dad and Dr. Dennis Wiles. First Baptist Church of Arlington called Dennis to be our pastor about eighteen months after my dad resigned. The decision to call Dennis and his family to our church has been one of the best decisions in the life of our church. He told us in his first sermon that he was "a Jesus man," and he has lived that out in front of us ever since. Many lives and families have been blessed as Dennis has served as our pastor. The Wade family is certainly one of those families. We love the Wiles family, and they love us. Our relationship is a special gift from God!

A few years ago, Dennis began to preach about the Psalm 1 tree. He directed our attention to Psalm 1:1-3. It speaks to the type of legacy and impact we can have as Christians if we stay true to His Word. We can become this "Psalm 1 tree" that is rooted in Christ and His Word. We can grow and branch out, providing shelter for others. We can bear spiritual fruit. As people need love, they pick that fruit off our branches. As they need joy, they take that piece of fruit.

As they need peace, patience, kindness, goodness, faithfulness, gentleness, and self-control, they look to us.

Now, to be sure, it is not us producing the fruit! It is the Holy Spirit, working through us, that produces fruit. As we learn and deepen our commitment to Love, Obey, Trust, and Serve, we bear L.O.T.S. of fruit. In so doing, our lives begin to be characterized by the fruit of the Spirit, and we leave a legacy of faith!

SCRIPTURE FOR TRUTH 13: OUR LIVES ARE CHARACTERIZED BY THE FRUIT OF THE SPIRIT

Read these Scriptures and reflect upon how Our Lives Are Characterized by the Fruit of the Spirit.

Blessed is the one who does not walk in step with the wicked or stand in the way that sinners take or sit in the company of mockers, but whose delight is in the law of the Lord, and who meditates on his law day and night. That person is like a tree planted by streams of water, which yields its fruit in season and whose leaf does not wither— whatever they do prospers. — Psalm 1:1-3

So I say, walk by the Spirit, and you will not gratify the desires of the flesh. — Galatians 5:16

But the fruit of the Spirit is love, joy, peace, forbearance, kindness, goodness, faithfulness, gentleness and self-control. Against such things there is no law. — Galatians 5:22-23

PRAY – READ – APPLY – MEMORIZE – SHARE

——————— DAY 1 ———————

Begin by praising the Lord of lords and the King of kings, the One who loved us enough to die for us, the One who teaches us all things and reminds us of all Jesus taught.

If you haven't already read through the introductory comments for Truth 13, read them now. Underline, highlight, or make notes in the margin as you read.

Read through the Scriptures for Truth 13.

Close with prayer.

——————— DAY 2 ———————

Open your time with God by thanking Him for the fruit of His Spirit. Thank the Holy Spirit for producing the fruit of love, joy, peace, patience, kindness, goodness, faithfulness, gentleness, and self-control in your life. Ask God to permeate your heart, your mind, and your deeds so His fruit in your life is healthy and on vivid display for His glory.

Read aloud the verses for Truth 13 and reflect upon how Our Lives Are Characterized by the Fruit of the Spirit. Which verses resonate with you most? Identify a verse to memorize this week. Write it down here and begin memorizing it.

Answer these questions. Pray and think about how you will apply them to your life.

- What shapes your perspective on life?

- How does your perspective shape your purpose and priorities?

- What are your priorities in life?

Close in prayer, asking God to reveal any amendments He would like you to make to the legacy you have envisioned for your life, and to guide you toward His holy perspective, purpose, and priorities for you.

——————— DAY 3 ———————

Look in the Psalms today for a verse or two of praise to open your time with God.

Read again the verses for this week.

Rehearse your memory verse.

Answer these questions. Pray and think about how you will apply them to your life.

- How would you describe your life in the context of Psalm 1:1-3?

- When people think of you, which fruit of the Spirit comes to their minds?

- Which fruit does not come to their mind?

Close by reading Psalm 1:1-3 and personalizing it as a prayer of commitment spoken to the Lord.

DAY 4

Try something new today! Open with a written prayer. Take a few moments to write below a few sentences of praise to the Father. If you find it difficult, imagine you are writing a letter of gratitude and thankfulness to your most faithful friend.

Read again the verses for this week.

Practice your memory verse.

Answer these questions. Pray and think about how you will apply them to your life.

- Which fruit in your life is healthy, ripe, and ready to be harvested?

- Which fruit needs more fertilizer and water?

- In what ways will you proactively prepare fruit for harvest?

Close your time with God by reading your written prayer aloud, adding other phrases and Scriptures to expand on your original prayer concepts.

———————— DAY 5 ————————

Begin your day by praising the One who made you, protected you, and gifted you. Offer your memory verse as a prayer to the Father.

Read again the verses for Truth 13.

Dig a little deeper into God's Word and find other passages that teach you about the Truth: Our Lives Are Characterized by the Fruit of the Spirit. List them here.

Pick your favorite verse from this week's Scriptures and pray it back to God today as you close in prayer.

———————— DAY 6 ————————

Refer to Psalm 71:1-6 and pray these words to the Father.

Read the verses for Truth 13 again.

Review your memory verse.

Answer these questions. Pray and think about how you will apply them to your life.

- What are some ways you can "fertilize" the fruit in your life that needs to mature?

- What kind of legacy do you want to leave?

Close by praying Psalm 71:22-23 to the Lord.

 **DAY 7**

If you are meeting with a small group as part of this study, use this day for your group meeting.

Here is a possible outline for your time together as a group:

Open Your Hearts

- WORSHIP SONG: "The Father's House" — Cory Asbury
- PRAYER: Encourage one or two people to offer a prayer of gratitude.
- SCRIPTURE: Ask one or two people to share the verse they memorized this week.

Discussion

1. What shapes your perspective on life, purpose, and priorities?

2. What are the priorities in your life?

3. Which fruit of the Spirit is the most mature in you?

4. Which needs more growing time?

5. What are some ways you can prepare spiritual fruit for harvest?

6. What legacy do you want to leave?

Time of Commitment

- WORSHIP SONG: "Will You Love Jesus More" — Phillips, Craig and Dean
- PRAYER: Have one or two people offer a prayer of commitment.

If you are not meeting with a small group, please take time on your own to go through the small group outline.

WE DIE TO LIVE
ETERNALLY WITH GOD

This journey to write *God in the Everyday* began with the news that my colleague, Don, had advanced stages of leukemia. Interestingly, just as I was preparing to write this section, I received a call from the wife of another longtime colleague, saying that her husband was on his deathbed.

Death. It will be here one day for all of us. Are we prepared?

My father-in-law, Mervin Childers, was prepared. He was ninety-one years old when he died. The latter years of his life were sweet and difficult at the same time. By the time he died, he had lost most of his short-term memory. In his last days, it was my privilege to help care for him. Prior to leaving the hospital, we would have conversations almost every morning that went like this:

"Mark, did you sleep well?"

"I did, Mr. C. How about you?"

"Oh, yes. I slept great and am feeling good. But, let me ask you, why are we here?"

"The doctors and nurses are trying to help you get strong enough so you can go home."

"Okay, that's good. They work hard here and are good people. I really appreciate all they're doing for me."

"You're right, Mr. C. They are taking good care of you."

"Is Ms. Genetty [his wife] okay?"

"Yes, sir. She's good. She's enjoying living in your new place at Brookdale."

"That's good. I'm glad we are there. Do you think she's going to be okay there?"

"Yes, sir. She's going to do great."

"Well, I'm glad about that. Now, how much is that costing us and are we going to be able to afford it?"

I would laugh and tell him how much and that, yes, they could afford it. Then he would say, "God has been good to us. I'm not a wealthy man but I'm not poor either. God has been faithful to provide and care for us all of our married life. I'm grateful."

He would be quiet and contemplative as he thought of God's faithfulness and provision for a few moments. Then he would say, "Mark, did you sleep well?" and the same conversation would repeat.

It was a sweet time for me. I loved him. Mr. C. mentored me and loved me from the time I was sixteen years old. From the very first day I met him, he had my respect. He was an example to me and everyone who knew him of what it meant to live an authentic life with God. Mr. C. was a man after God's heart. He loved Jesus. His perspectives and priorities were all shaped by his relationship with Jesus. He loved his wife, his two girls, and his three grandsons. He battled the difficulties of life with dignity, courage, and hope. He served our country in World War II as a Marine. He never allowed himself to embrace a victim mentality that wondered why something bad was happening or why God wasn't making it all better. Mr. C. always looked at life, the good times and the difficult times, as a gift from God. Therefore, when it came time for him to leave this world and live eternally with Jesus, he was ready! He was grateful for the life he had lived and was looking forward to the eternal life he would live with Jesus.

What we believe about Jesus changes everything… in this life and the life to come! I pray you know Him. I pray you know the peace and courage that comes with an authentic, growing, daily, healthy relationship with Christ. There is no more important decision than what you will do with Jesus. Will you accept Him and ask Him to lead your life, or will you reject Him? When you reject Jesus, you reject His claim to be the Son of the Living God, His gift of Himself to die in your place, His forgiveness of your sins, and His offer to make a way for you to live eternally with Him.

The choice is simple: choose Jesus as Lord and Savior or choose to reject Him as Lord and Savior. You may accept that He is God's Son yet refuse to ask Him to save you and be Lord of your life. Please don't make that mistake. The consequences are staggering…gargantuan…eternal!

> *When the Son of Man comes in his glory, and all the angels with him, he will sit on his glorious throne. All the nations will be gathered before him, and he will separate the people one from another as a shepherd separates the sheep from the goats. He will put the sheep on his right and the goats on his left. Then the King will say to those on his right, "Come, you who are blessed by my Father; take your inheritance, the kingdom prepared for you since the creation of the world. For I was hungry and you gave me something to eat, I was thirsty and you gave me something to drink, I was a stranger and you invited me in, I needed clothes and you clothed me, I was sick and you looked after me, I was in prison and you came to visit me." Then the righteous will answer him, "Lord, when did we see you hungry and feed you, or thirsty and give you something to drink? When did we see you a stranger and invite you in, or needing clothes and clothe you? When did we see you sick or in prison and go to visit you?" The King will reply, "Truly I tell you, whatever you did for one of the least of these brothers and sisters of mine, you did for me." Then he will say to those on his left, "Depart from me, you who are cursed, into the eternal fire prepared for the devil and his angels. For I was hungry and you gave me nothing to eat, I was thirsty and you gave me nothing to drink, I was a stranger and you did not invite me in, I needed clothes and you did not clothe me, I was sick and in prison and you did not look after me." They also will answer, "Lord, when did we see you hungry or thirsty or a stranger or needing clothes or sick or in prison, and did not help you?" He will reply, "Truly I tell you, whatever you did not do for one of the least of these, you did not do for me." Then they will go away to eternal punishment, but the righteous to eternal life. (Matthew 25:31-46)*

Choose Jesus as Lord of your life. Follow Him. Serve Him. Live eternally with Him. Are you still not sure? Trust what the Word of God says!

SCRIPTURE FOR TRUTH 14:
WE DIE TO LIVE ETERNALLY WITH GOD

---

*Read these Scriptures and reflect upon
how We Die to Live Eternally with God.*

The LORD is my shepherd, I lack nothing. He makes me lie down in green pastures, he leads me beside quiet waters, He refreshes my soul. He guides me along the right paths for his name's sake. Even though I walk through the darkest valley, I will fear no evil, for you are with me; your rod and your staff, they comfort me. You prepare a table before me in the presence of my enemies. You anoint my head with oil; my cup overflows. Surely your goodness and love will follow me all the days of my life, and I will dwell in the house of the LORD forever. — Psalm 23

When the perishable has been clothed with the imperishable, and the mortal with immortality, then the saying that is written will come true: "Death has been swallowed up in victory." "Where, O death, is your victory? Where, O death, is your sting?" — 1 Corinthians 15:54-56

For God so loved the world that he gave his one and only Son, that whoever believes in him shall not perish but have eternal life. — John 3:16

Very truly I tell you, whoever hears my word and believes him who sent me has eternal life and will not be judged but has crossed over from death to life. — John 5:24

For my Father's will is that everyone who looks to the Son and believes in him shall have eternal life, and I will raise them up at the last day. — John 6:40

Jesus said to her, "I am the resurrection and the life. The one who believes in me will live, even though they die; and whoever lives by believing in me will never die." — John 11:25-26

But now that you have been set free from sin and have become slaves of God, the benefit you reap leads to holiness, and the result is eternal life. — Romans 6:22

His master replied, well done, good and faithful servant! You have been faithful with a few things; I will put you in charge of many things. Come and share your master's happiness! —Matthew 25:21

For the Lord himself will come down from heaven, with a loud command, with the voice of the archangel and with the trumpet call of God, and the dead in Christ will rise first. After that, we who are still alive and are left will be caught up together with them in the clouds to meet the Lord in the air. And so we will be with the Lord forever. — 1 Thessalonians 4:16-17

PRAY - READ - APPLY - MEMORIZE - SHARE

—————— DAY 1 ——————

Praise the Father for who He is, was, and will forever be. He spoke and all things came into being. He breathed the breath of life into every living creature. He created you exactly as He intended. Today, thank Him for life. Thank Him for walking every day with you.

If you haven't chosen Jesus as Lord of your life, ask Him to be Lord of your life right now. Choose Jesus. Thank Him for His saving power. Thank Him for defeating sin, death, and the grave so that you can live with him today and every day to come—in this life and in life eternal.

If you haven't already read through the introductory comments for Truth 14, read them now. Underline, highlight, or make notes in the margin as you read.

Read through the Scriptures for Truth 14.

Close by praying Psalm 16:11 to God.

—————— DAY 2 ——————

Open your prayer time by reading Psalm 36:9-10 to the Lord.

Read aloud the Scriptures for Truth 14 and reflect upon how We Die to Live Eternally with God. Which verses resonate with you most? Identify a verse to memorize this week. Write it down here and begin memorizing it.

Answer these questions. Pray and think about how you are able to apply them to your life.

- Have you asked Jesus to be Lord and Savior of your life?

- If you have not, what is keeping you from doing so?

- Will you ask Him to be Lord of your life right now?

Close in prayer, thanking God for extending to each of us His personal invitation to forgiveness and eternal life.

DAY 3

Open your Bible and turn to Galatians 6:14. Read it several times, highlighting the key words in the verse. Now begin your time with God with a prayer of deep gratitude for His gift of salvation to you.

Read again the Scriptures for this week.

Rehearse your memory verse.

Answer these questions. Pray and think about how you are able to apply them to your life.

- If you have asked Jesus to be Lord of your life, are you living a life worthy of Him?

- What does it mean to live a life worthy of Him?

Close in prayer.

———— DAY 4 ————

Look through the Psalms and find a new verse to open your prayer time today. Write it here.

Read the Scriptures again for this week.

Practice your memory verse.

Answer these questions. Pray and think about how you are able to apply them to your life.

- How does your life point people to Jesus?

- What needs to change in your life so that you consistently and authentically point others to Jesus?

Consider what you wrote on the last question and center your closing prayer time around relinquishing your hold on the things that keep you from being the disciple God is calling you to be.

—————— DAY 5 ——————

Start your day praising God for who He is and thanking Him for all He has and is doing in your life. Offer your memory verse as a part of your prayer.

Read again the verses for Truth 14.

Dig a little deeper into God's Word and find other passages that teach you about the Truth: We Die to Live Eternally with God. List them here:

Pick your favorite verse from this week's Scriptures and pray it back to God today as you close in prayer.

—————— DAY 6 ——————

Open with prayer. Consider singing or humming a song of praise that comes to mind.

Read the Scriptures for Truth 14 again.

Review your memory verse.

Answer these questions. Pray and think about how you are able to apply them to your life.

- This week, you have thought about what is keeping you from being wholly faithful to God in the everyday. Can you identify specific distractions that need to be removed, wrong priorities that need to change, or sin that needs to be rooted out? List them here.

- Consider Paul's words in Galatians 2:20: "*I have been crucified with Christ and I no longer live, but Christ lives in me. The life I now live in the body, I live by faith in the Son of God, who loved me and gave himself for me.*" What do you need to symbolically crucify so that it no longer holds you hostage from living the fullest life God has for you?

Close in prayer, making complete your commitment to relinquish these things.

————————— DAY 7 —————————

If you are meeting with a small group as part of this study, use this day for your group meeting.

Here is a possible outline for your time together as a group:

Open Your Hearts

- WORSHIP SONG: "It is Well" — Hillsong

- PRAYER: Ask one or two people to offer a prayer of gratitude.

- SCRIPTURE: Encourage one or two people to share the verse they memorized this week.

Discussion

1. Read Ephesians 4:1-6 and Colossians 1:9-12. What does it mean to "*live a life worthy of the calling you have received*"?

2. How does your life point people to Jesus?

3. This week, you have thought about what is keeping you from being wholly devoted to Jesus. Share specific distractions that need to be removed, wrong priorities that need to change, or sin that needs to be rooted out.

4. Share with the group progress you have made toward being wholly devoted to Jesus. Share what you have relinquished, given up, or symbolically crucified.

5. Read aloud all of the Scriptures for this Truth. As a group, discuss what Truth 14 presents about the idea of life after death. Has your view on death changed or matured as a result of this Truth? Does death still scare you? If so, what about it scares you?

6. If dying is not fearful for you, share the journey you have traveled that helped you reach this level of peace about death.

7. Read the "Conclusion" and "What to Do Next" sections as a way of wrapping up your small group study of *God in the Everyday*. Commit to:

   • Identifing four or five Scriptures that will help you have the wisdom, courage, and discipline to make decisions that put a smile on God's face, decisions that will honor Him in every part of your life

   • Writing the Scriptures down

   • Posting them where you can see them each day

   • Praying these Scriptures and embedding them in your heart and in your mind

Time of Commitment

- WORSHIP SONG: "I Can Only Imagine" — MercyMe

- PRAYER: Offer prayers of gratitude for the assurance of life with God in the everyday—in this physical life as well as life eternal with the Father.

If you are not meeting with a small group, please take time on your own to go through the small group outline.

A PRAYER
OF BLESSING

In conclusion, I will pose the same question with which we began. What does the Bible say about living life with God in the everyday? My prayer is that you see and embrace the following 14 Truths, learning to seek God every day, to live obediently, and to trust Him completely:

- Everything begins with God.
- God gives us life.
- God gives us abilities that grow and mature.
- We recognize our sin.
- We meet Jesus.
- We choose Jesus.
- We receive the Holy Spirit.
- We receive spiritual gifts.
- We are equipped to continue the work of Jesus and grow His Kingdom.
- We exercise our gifts in obedience and love.
- We grow in the Lord experiencing spiritual formation and maturity.

- Our gifts develop and we bear fruit.

- Our lives are characterized by the fruit of the Spirit.

- We die to live eternally with God.

Eugene Peterson, in *The Message*, paraphrases Romans 12:1-2 this way:

> *So here's what I want you to do, God helping you: Take your everyday, ordinary life—your sleeping, eating, going-to-work, and walking-around life—and place it before God as an offering. Embracing what God does for you is the best thing you can do for him. Don't become so well-adjusted to your culture that you fit into it without even thinking. Instead, fix your attention on God. You'll be changed from the inside out. Readily recognize what he wants from you, and quickly respond to it. Unlike the culture around you, always dragging you down to its level of immaturity, God brings the best out of you, develops well-formed maturity in you.*

Let me encourage you: pursue this incredible journey I call living life with God in the everyday. It is a journey you absolutely, positively don't want to miss. It will bless you more than you can ask or even imagine, and it will likewise bless the people with whom you connect.

I offer this prayer of blessing for you and your family:

> *May the Lord bless you and keep you.*
>
> *May He turn His face toward you and smile upon you.*
>
> *May His strong, protective arms be wrapped tightly around you.*
>
> *May He teach you to love Him with all your heart, soul, mind, and strength.*
>
> *May He teach you to love others as He loves them.*
>
> *May He grant you wisdom of the heart and wisdom in the moment.*
>
> *May the hand of His provision be open wide.*
>
> *May the joy of His salvation, the strength of His character, and the fellowship of His Spirit rest upon you this day and every day forever more.*
>
> *Amen.*

WHAT TO DO NEXT?

When we accept Jesus' forgiveness and ask Him to be Lord of our lives, we embark on a journey of living life with Him in the everyday, and it becomes a journey for all eternity. It begins the moment we respond to the prompting of the Holy Spirit and choose Jesus, and it never ends. Let's try to wrap our minds around that truth… not one minute of any day, in this life and the life to come, do we live without Jesus!

As we travel this journey, we learn to love God more and more. The desire to obey Him and please Him deepens. We want our decisions to put a smile on His face and to bring Him honor in all we do. And I'm not just talking about the big decisions of life. I'm not just talking about certain decisions. I'm talking about *every* decision.

- How should I treat other people?
- How do I treat myself?
- Should I do this or do that?
- Should I take that job or keep this job?
- What is the solution?
- What is the right thing to do?

How do we make the right decision every time? The short answer is we don't. We can't. We are human. However, we can dramatically reduce the number of bad decisions and increase the number of good decisions.

How?

My experience is that we plant Scripture deep in our hearts: Scripture that will give us guidance at the point of every decision, Scripture that speaks of His character, Scripture that lays the framework for living life with Him in the everyday, and Scripture that not only gives us wisdom to know the right decision but also the courage and discipline to do what's right, regardless.

A number of years ago, I adopted four Scriptures to help me make the right decisions and to have the courage and discipline to follow through. Do I always make the right decisions? Of course not. At the same time, having these Scriptures as a part of my everyday prayer life gives me more of His power to make decisions that please Him.

- Love the Lord with all my heart, soul, mind, and strength (Mark 12:30).

- Love others as Jesus loves them (John 13:34; 15:12).

- Seek Him and work wholeheartedly (2 Chronicles 31:21).

- Trust Him to do immeasurably more than all I can ask or even imagine according to His power which is at work in me (Ephesians 3:20).

Now it's your turn. Review the Scriptures contained in this material, as well as others you identified throughout your study. Select four or five Scriptures to give you the wisdom, courage, and discipline to make decisions that will put a smile on God's face, decisions that will honor Him in every part of your life. Write these Scriptures below. Post them where you can see them each day. As you live life with Him in the everyday, pray these Scriptures and embed them in your heart and in your mind.

1.

2.

3.

4.

5.

What will happen along this daily journey?

- You will LOVE more deeply.

- You will OBEY more quickly.

- You will TRUST more completely.

- You will SERVE more cheerfully... out of who you are becoming, your personhood... in your home, with your friends, in the marketplace, in your church, everywhere you go... influencing well and bearing L.O.T.S. of healthy fruit.

Join me in choosing commitment to Love, Obey, Trust, and Serve. Join me in choosing commitment to living life with God in the Everyday. Hope, purpose, and fulfillment will meet you along the journey.

ABOUT THE AUTHOR

C. Mark Wade has been a Bible study leader for high school students, college students, and young adults for over 30 years and has served in many capacities in his local church. A sales coach by profession, Mark and his wife, Pam, live in Arlington, Texas. They have two adult sons. Discover more about Mark's passion for discipleship at choosecommitment.org.

NOTES

1. Stott, John. "Pride, Humility & God". Sovereign Grace Online. *C.S. Lewis Institute.* [Online] September/October 2000. https://www.cslewisinstitute.org/webfm_send/375.

2. Nouwen, Henri. An Invitation to the Spiritual Life. *Christianity Today.* [Online] Summer 1981. https://www.christianitytoday.com/pastors/1981/summer/81l3053.html.

3. *Ministry Essentials Bible, New International Version.* Peabody : Hendrickson Publishers, 2014. pp. 1874-1875.

4. 15 Facts About the Human Body! National Geographic Kids Science. *National Geographis Kids.* [Online] www.natgeokids.com/nz/discover/science/general-science/15-facts-about-the-human-body/.

5. Long, Kat. 25 Amazing Facts About the Human Body. Mental Floss Lists. *Mental Floss.* [Online] March 19, 2019. www.mentalfloss.com/article/570937/facts-about-the-human-body.

6. 10 Cool Facts About the Human Body. MedPro Disposal Practice Management. *MedPro Disposal.* [Online] June 30, 2017. www.medprodisposal.com/10-cool-facts-about-the-human-body.

7. Lewis, Tanya. Human Brain: Facts, Functions and Anatomy. Live Science References. *Live Science.* [Online] September 28, 2018. www.livescience.com/29365-human-brain.html.

8. Dudley-Smith, Timothy. *John Stott, The Making of a Leader.* Leicester : Inter-Varsity Press, 1999. p. 95.

9. BibleGateway. *biblegateway.com.* [Online] [Cited: May 28, 2021.] https://www.biblegateway.com/quicksearch/?quicksearch.

10. BibleGateway. *biblegateway.com.* [Online] [Cited: May 28, 2021.] https://www.biblegateway.com/quicksearch/?quicksearch.

11. Maxwell, John. *The Maxwell Leadership Bible, Second Edition.* Nashville : Thomas Nelson, 2002, 2007. p. 631.

12. Ralston, Lance. Marks of a Great Leader: Servant vs Service. Christian Vision Alliance Marks of a Great Leader: Servant vs Service. *Christian Vision Alliance.* [Online] May 31, 2017. www.livescience.com/29365-human-brain.html.

13. Mother Teresa, Jose Luis Gonzalez-Balado. *In My Own Words.* New York : Barnes & Noble Books, 1996. p. 1.

14. *Life Application Study Bible, New International Version.* Carol Stream : Tyndale House, 1988, 1989, 1990, 1991, 1993, 1996, 2004, 2005. p. 984.

15. Maxwell, John. *The Maxwell Leadership Bible, Second Edition.* Nashville : Thomas Nelson, 2002, 2007. p. 1190.

16. Moran, Brian P. *The 12 Week Year.* Hoboken : John Wiley & Sons, Inc., 2013. p. 58.

17. Maxwell, John. *The Maxwell Leadership Bible, Second Edition.* Nashville : Thomas Nelson, 2002, 2007. p. 1538.

CPSIA information can be obtained
at www.ICGtesting.com
Printed in the USA
FSHW020139230721
83460FS